The C-5A Scandal

Books by Berkeley Rice

Enter Gambia:
The Birth of an Improbable Nation
The Other End of the Leash:
The American Way with Pets
The C-5A Scandal:
An Inside Story of the Military-Industrial Complex

The
C-5A
Scandal

An Inside Story of
the Military-Industrial Complex

Berkeley Rice

Houghton Mifflin Company
Boston   1971

First Printing c

International Standard Book Number:
0-395-12103-5
Library of Congress Catalog Card Number:
73-144075
Printed in the United States of America

Dedication

This book is dedicated to the few public servants who tried to protect the public's interest during the C–5A affair: Ernest Fitzgerald, Senator William Proxmire, Representative Otis Pike, Representative William Moorhead, Richard Kaufman, and Peter Stockton. Without their efforts, the public might never have heard of the C–5A scandal, and this book could not have been written.

Acknowledgments

Although military affairs consume nearly half the federal budget, American journalism has devoted remarkably little attention to the subject of military procurement. In the case of the C–5A, however, a few publications covered the story well, and occasionally contributed to it: *The Washington Post, The Wall Street Journal, Armed Forces Journal, The New Republic,* and *The Nation.* I would also like to express my gratitude and respect to those reporters and columnists who helped expose the C–5A scandal: Bernard Nossiter, Patrick Sloyan, Mary McGrory, I. F. Stone, Jack Anderson, James Phillips, Robert Sherrill, and Murray Kempton.

I would like to thank the Fund for Investigative Journalism for its generous support of much of the research that went into this book.

Contents

Introduction

A FORMER EDITOR of mine, appalled by the number of books being published these days, used to grumble that most of them should have been articles or chapters. *The C–5A Scandal*, despite his advice, is a chapter that became a book. I had set out to write a book about the military-industrial complex — not just another attack on it, but an attempt to show in detail how it really functions. The C–5A affair was to be only a chapter, a shocking example of defense contracting. As I learned more about this giant military cargo transport, however, I realized how dramatically it illustrates all the problems of the entire defense procurement system. Nearly everything that could possibly happen to a major defense program happened to the C–5A: political pressure, gross mismanagement, enormous waste, confusion.

I could have chosen other major defense programs like the Minuteman missile or the F–111 to illustrate these problems, but none of them can match the C–5A in scope, and none have caused such a public scandal. The C–5A Galaxy is not only the largest, most expensive airplane in the world, it represents one of the most costly defense contracts in military history. Each of the plane's engines and each wing cost more than $1 million.

The price of each plane has risen from the 1965 contract estimate of $20 million apiece to nearly $60 million. The cost of the total program has risen from an original estimate of $3 billion for 115 planes to somewhere around $5 billion for only 81. Because of the complexity of the contract, no one really knows yet, despite numerous cost studies, what the final price of the C–5A program will be — not the Lockheed Aircraft Corporation, which builds them, not the Air Force, which ordered them, and least of all the public, which will pay for them.

According to the reams of press releases spewed out by publicity people at Lockheed and the Pentagon, the C–5A should be a marvel of aerospace technology. However, although the Air Force has already accepted delivery on the planes, they have yet to demonstrate many of the marvelous capabilities described in the press releases. Their actual performance has been so poor that some critics have referred to them as "lemons." Among their defects (or "bugs," as the PR men call them) have been such items as wings that cracked and wheels that fell off.

Somehow the Air Force managed to hide the C–5A's defects and the $2 billion cost overrun from Congress and the public until quite recently, when it was too late for anyone to do much about them. When Senator William Proxmire tried to learn how the Air Force had accomplished this feat, he found "a pattern of inconsistencies, concealment, failure to disclose information, and manipulation of records." What Congress did do, once the cost overrun became a public scandal, shows how well Congress serves as an active partner in the military-industrial complex.

Until the exposure of this $2 billion overrun, the Pentagon had hailed the C–5A program as a model of modern defense contracting. Today, critics like Senator Proxmire call it "one of the greatest fiscal disasters in the history of military contracting." It has brought Lockheed, the nation's largest defense contractor, perilously close to bankruptcy. Public revelations of this disaster have led to investigations of the C–5A program by Proxmire's Subcommittee on Economy in Government, the Senate and House Armed Services Committees, the House Military Operations Subcommittee, the General Accounting Office, and the Securities and Exchange Commission. Despite all these investigations, however, neither the Pentagon, Congress, nor the Nixon administration has done much about the C–5A. The chief reason for such inaction is that despite all the publicity there has been little public pressure to do so. Most Americans merely read about the C–5A scandal in the papers and shrugged.

To the average citizen, whose major financial concerns range from the price of a new car to a home mortgage, $5 billion or even $5 million are relatively meaningless figures. They seem like fairly large amounts of money, but then so do most sums the federal government deals with. Even in Washington, D.C., however, $5,000,000,000 represents a great deal of money — more than the combined budgets of Congress and the Departments of State, Justice, Interior, and Commerce. The cost of the C–5A program alone is nearly twice as much as all federal aid to public schools in 1970; nearly three times the budget for all federal poverty programs; three times as much as all federal expenditures on public health programs; more than five times as much as the federal government spends on low and moderate-income housing; more than five times what it spends on law enforcement, justice, and civil rights; nearly 15 times the money devoted to the nation's parks and recreation facilities; and 50 times as much as the federal funds available for mass urban transit. Until the nation's taxpayers begin to think in such terms, and realize what defense dollars could do for the rest of the country's problems, they will not care whether they are getting their money's worth out of the Pentagon. And as long as the public doesn't care, the Pentagon and Congress won't either.

The C–5A scandal did generate enough embarrassing publicity to worry some officials at the Defense Department, but like officials in any government agency beset by scandal, they merely appointed commissions and ordered numerous studies, reports, and policy reviews. Basically nothing has changed, because the Pentagon, Congress, and the public mistakenly concluded that the troubles with the C–5A program were peculiar to the C–5A. Unfortunately they are common to most major defense procurement programs. The C–5A is merely a symptom of a disease that runs throughout the entire military-industrial complex. The problem is not the plane, but the system. Scandalous as it is, the C–5A is by no means the worst example of defense contracting. Many military projects have cost overruns of several hundred per cent. Some Air Force officials in fact still insist the C–5A represents "the best cost history we have ever had on any major program." If so, I hope *The C–5A Scandal* makes the reader wonder about the others.

This book shows that the Pentagon's best, or even normal manner of spending public money is incredibly sloppy. It shows that the military-industrial complex is institutionally incapable of either thrift or efficiency. It shows how the Pentagon and its defense contractors regularly manage to conceal enormous cost overruns. It shows how the Pentagon suppresses internal criticism, and punishes anyone who tries to expose the waste or reform the system. It shows that most of those in Congress responsible for guarding the public's investment in defense are either uninformed or uninterested in doing so, and that some of them actually contribute to the waste. It shows that except for a few dedicated public servants, the American people are nearly defenseless against the power of the Pentagon and its allies in Congress and the defense industry.

The C-5A Scandal

CHAPTER ONE

The Birth of the Galaxy

*"There's more porkbarrel than strategic need to the
Galaxy."*

Howard Atherton,
Mayor of Marietta, Georgia

No ONE, not even the publicity people at Lockheed, would call
the Galaxy graceful. Parked before its hangar the plane resembles
a beached whale, leading *Newsweek* to dub it "Moby Jet." On
takeoffs it lumbers down the runway like a bloated pigeon. On
short landings its wings flap like those of a frightened pelican.
But the Galaxy was not built for beauty. Its virtues are functional
rather than visual — measured not by the eye, but with the slide
rule and the computer. It claims our attention by its awesome
size, cost, and, at least on paper, performance.

It is difficult to describe the sheer size of the C–5A in words.
One should stand beneath the behemoth and feel its bulk looming
above, blocking out the sky. The Galaxy is not merely huge —
it is a public relations man's dream. Only 18 yards shorter than
a football field, it has a 223-foot wing span and a tail six stories
high. Its four 16-foot, 7000-pound turbofan jet engines are twice
as powerful as any in existence and could furnish electricity for a
city of 50,000 people. Its cavernous fuselage can swallow 14
jet fighters, 50 Cadillacs, or any 250,000-pound assortment of
tanks, helicopters, cannons, trucks, or other equipment.

Despite its massive size the Galaxy reportedly handles easily, climbs quickly, and reaches speeds over 600 miles per hour. According to its specifications, it can perform all sorts of marvelous feats in the way of transporting cargo. Carrying twice the payload of the next largest military cargo plane, it can theoretically fly nearly 3000 miles, land, unload, and take off on a 4000-foot dirt runway (a Boeing 707 needs 10,000 feet on a normal runway), and return to its base without refueling — all under weather conditions that would shut down civilian airports. The C–5A can supposedly operate at temperatures ranging from an Arctic 65 degrees below zero to the steaming 120 degree heat of Southeast Asia. A built-in "malfunction detector" is supposed to electronically monitor 600 test points, locate any troubles, and print out repair instructions.

Of all the Galaxy's virtues, many of which are still unproven in actual operation, Pentagon logistics men are particularly impressed by some special features designed to permit the plane to operate into primitive landing strips that have no mechanical facilities for unloading. The C–5A's 28 tires can be deflated in-flight for landing on unpaved runways, and in an emergency the pilot can bring this hulk to a screeching halt in only 500 yards — less than six times its own length. It can lower itself nearly three feet for loading and unloading, and wheeled cargo can simply drive up or down its built-in ramps. Because its bulbous nose swings up on hinges like the yawning maw of some prehistoric monster, the plane can disgorge its cargo at both ends, cutting the normal load-unload time in half. All of these features enable the C–5A to land, unload, and take off in one hour, with no need for ground support. This time element is extremely critical in forward battle zones such as those being regularly supplied by air in Vietnam. There the enemy is often within easy mortar range of the airstrip, and a plane that unloads too slowly may never take off again.

*

Talk of a giant jet transport began to be heard around the Pentagon by 1962, early in the reign of Defense Secretary Robert McNamara. With a fleet of such planes, proponents argued, the United States would be able to deploy fully equipped forces around the world on a day's notice. To the cost-conscious Mc-Namara regime this meant reducing the need for large contingents of U.S. troops stationed abroad, thereby cutting the balance of payments deficit as well as defense costs. (No one talked much then about the cost of the plane itself.) Most important, this capability of immediate massive intervention would supposedly mean a more flexible response to brush-fire wars and other strategic threats. It would give the U.S. a "remote presence" anywhere in the world.[1]

Flexibility is a nice word for the kind of military options the C–5A offers. Just 12 of them could have handled the entire Berlin Airlift, which required 224 planes in 1948. A fleet of 100 C–5As, according to the Pentagon's planners, could transport 15,000 combat troops, including all their equipment, from the U.S. to Europe in 24 hours. As one Defense Department official noted happily, "This will mean an Army division in Kansas is just as much on the front lines as one in Germany." A high-ranking Air Force officer claims the C–5A will "largely determine the mobility of our forces during the 1970's and 1980's."

However pleased Defense officials are with the prospect of such massive mobility, there are those who fear it will mean more frequent and even less reasoned or justifiable U.S. military interventions than in the past. The C–5A's critics claim all the talk about remote presence and flexible response can be translated into a modern form of gunboat diplomacy, or "Pax Americana." As evidence, they might well point to Lockheed's trade ads, aimed largely at DoD and military officials. In them, the company proudly describes the C–5A as "more than the world's largest airplane. It's a new kind of defense system. It's like having a military base in nearly every strategic spot on the globe."

While the prospect of such geographic omnipotence may please Lockheed and the Pentagon, it worries men like Senator William Fulbright, chairman of the Senate Foreign Relations Committee. In June, 1969, he expressed his fears before a Joint Economic Committee hearing on U.S. defense policy. "If we get enough C–5A's," said Fulbright, "and if they should happen to fly once they are made, we could send enormous numbers [of troops] any-where overnight . . . If we have big planes which will, on a moment's notice, take two or three divisions to every outbreak that may occur, wherever it may be, we will be tempted to do it. . . . But I don't think we ought to be projecting our military power all over the world, and undertaking to settle every quarrel that breaks out anywhere . . . I do not think we have the wis-dom and the experience and the manpower to run the world, and to keep the peace in that sense." [2]

Most officials over at the Pentagon would probably disagree with Senator Fulbright on this subject, particularly those in the Army. During the 1950s, when theories of massive retaliation and atomic warfare dominated strategic thinking around the Pentagon, the Army began to feel lost and unneeded. Most of the new hardware was being handled by the Air Force, and no one seemed to talk much about the need for ground troops any-more. Under the leadership of General Maxwell Taylor, along with other airborne-oriented officers, the Army began to empha-size its role in limited wars. When General Taylor became military adviser to President John Kennedy, the Army had its spokesman in an excellent strategic position. To airlift troops and heavy equipment to brush-fire wars, however, the Army had to have bigger and faster planes than the C–124s and C–130s in stock at the time. Hence the C–5A.

With the support of both the Army and the Air Force, which would handle the contract and supervise the plane's construction, the Defense Department finally in 1964 decided to go ahead with the C–5A. Informal briefings with prospective bidders for the prime contract to build and assemble the plane narrowed the field down to three companies: Boeing; Lockheed-Georgia, a division of Lockheed Aircraft; and Douglas Aircraft, since merged into McDonnell Douglas Corporation. While such a winnowing process may seem arbitrary to the layman, it is not necessarily evidence of any conspiracy to restrain trade. At least not at this point. The C–5A contract would be one of the largest in military history. The awesome physical, financial, and technological capabilities required to produce such a gigantic aircraft automatically eliminate all but a very few of the largest aerospace firms. Of course the process does have an unhealthy effect upon what used to be known as the free enterprise system, since only those companies that have previously held such contracts can afford to develop and maintain the technical manpower and production facilities necessary to compete successfully for subsequent major contracts. Partly for this reason, the list of the ten largest defense contractors varies little from one year to the next. Lockheed, for example, has been first or second on this list for nine of the last ten years.

Of the three companies selected to compete for the C–5A, Boeing was easily in the best shape, since it already had about a thousand men at work on plans for such a giant jet plane — now its 747 — and had been trying to talk the Air Force into the idea for some time. Lockheed, still heavily committed to an earlier DoD contract, had to scramble to assemble a several-hundred-man design-engineering team for its proposal.

In May, 1964, the formal minuet of defense contracting began with an Air Force request for preliminary conceptual studies.

The three firms submitted plans, received study contracts in June, and had their initial designs in by September. In December, 1964, the "contract definition" phase of the process opened with the Air Force request for proposals (RFP), a 1500-page document full of detailed specifications. Again the three firms submitted proposals and the Air Force accepted them and awarded contracts for the preparation of final bids.

During this bid-formulation phase, Boeing, Lockheed, and Douglas had a total of nearly 6000 men working full time on the engineering, production, and cost problems involved in the C–5A contract. They not only had to prepare their own technical and cost data, but also had to line up hundreds of subcontractors for the plane's parts and systems, and fix them to a firm delivery schedule. In order to prepare their proposals for the prime contractors, these subcontractors in turn had to negotiate with the hundreds of smaller companies that supply them. And so on.

At this point some readers may be wondering how Boeing, Lockheed, and Douglas could afford to gamble so many high-priced man-hours on a proposal with no guarantee of success. Do not worry. The Air Force paid them (and the two bidders on the separate engine contract) a total of $61 million for their trouble. In the good old days of rugged free enterprise, companies often did risk sizable investments in the preparation of bids on large defense contracts, just as they still do on most commercial contracts. Some of the losers went broke in the process, or were swallowed up by more successful competitors. Today, however, the financial resources necessary for bidding on multi-billion dollar defense contracts are too great to risk on a gamble. So the Defense Department removes most of the risk by subsidizing or "funding" much of the bidding process. Sic transit capitalism.

Whatever money the companies commit to the bidding process beyond their government subsidies can easily be justified. First of all they must continue to win major contracts in order to stay in the defense business. The fate of Douglas Aircraft presents a perfect illustration of how this survival of the fittest occurs in the defense industry. Shortly after, and obviously as a result of losing out on its bid for the C–5A contract, Douglas was absorbed by McDonnell Corporation, another aircraft manufacturer. In the polite language of corporate public relations, this acquisition is referred to as a "merger."

In the case of the C–5A contract, the motivation was much stronger than the mere desire to stay in business. As *Fortune* magazine pointed out at the time, Boeing, Lockheed, and Douglas were "aware that the stakes were appreciably greater than the program itself. The winners could expect to get a corner on the commercial market for a plane that promises eventually to become a standard workhorse of the air transport business." [3] The winner of the C–5A contract, in effect, would be financed by the Air Force while it developed the necessary technical and production experience for a potentially far more profitable commercial plane. Because of this the competition for the C–5A contract became what *Business Week* called "the most strenuous in aerospace history."

Competition between Boeing, Lockheed, and Douglas for control of the commercial aircraft market goes back more than two decades. Since Lockheed ceased production of its Constellations, in the era of piston-driven propeller engines, its share of that market had dropped off sharply. In the 1950s Lockheed executives, guessing that the airlines were not yet ready for a plunge into straight jets, decided to develop the turboprop Electra. They guessed wrong, however, and the airlines began ordering jet aircraft from Boeing (the 707) and Douglas (the DC–8). Because of this miscalculation, and the fact that two passenger-laden Electras crashed soon after beginning service, Lockheed sold only 176 of them to the airlines. Later, the company redesigned the plane for military use and managed to sell 200 of them, mostly to the Navy as long-range patrol planes.

About 1955–56 Lockheed-Georgia developed the C–130 Hercules, a highly dependable and effective aircraft that has been its bread-and-butter product for more than a decade, and the U.S. military's standard cargo plane. The Defense Department has bought more than 1000 C–130s at an average price of $2.3 million each (less than 5 per cent of the cost of a C–5A). The "Herky Bird" proved its durable versatility again during the Vietnam war, particularly when it was used to supply the beleaguered mountaintop Marine garrison at Khesanh. No other plane of comparable capacity could get in and out of Khesanh's 3800-foot dirt runway.

Valuable as the C–130's virtues are to the military, however, they have been largely responsible for its lack of commercial appeal. Today's cargo airlines fly to very few short dirt runways and rarely have to unload while the plane is still taxiing, or drop their cargo by parachute. The Hercules has remained primarily a military plane, leaving Lockheed with no major entry in the commercial aircraft market.

As a successor to the C–130, the Pentagon, in 1960, asked for a bigger, pure jet air freighter. This time, the assumption was that such a plane could be designed to satisfy commercial as well as military requirements, in order to provide the Defense Department with a civilian reserve of militarily useful planes and crews. When Lockheed-Georgia beat out Boeing and Douglas for this contract too, they charged that the decision had been influenced by two very influential Georgians: Senator Richard Russell, then chairman of the Senate Armed Services Committee, and Representative Carl Vinson, then chairman of the House Armed Services Committee. Certainly their support did nothing to hurt Lockheed's bid, but the Pentagon's decision may have also hinged on the company's impressive record with the C–130.

Though Lockheed won this battle, it lost out again in the commercial market. While it was developing and producing the new plane — called the C–141 Starlifter — Boeing and Douglas went back and designed cargo versions of their biggest passenger jets, which have since become the standard commercial air freighters today. Adding to Lockheed's woes, the Defense Department never ordered more than the 284 Starlifters included in the first contract and Lockheed never sold any to the airlines.

Soon after the first Starlifters began military service, a major limitation became apparent — one which should have been embarrassing to the Pentagon officials who planned its specifications. With military equipment rapidly growing in size, they discovered that roughly one third of an Army division's current paraphernalia would not fit through the doors of a C–141. At the same time, the development of the high compression turbofan or fan-jet engine, with its greater thrust-to-weight ratio, created the prospect of a cargo plane much larger and heavier than the Starlifter — namely, the C–5A Galaxy.

By the time of the C–5A bidding in 1965, Lockheed-Georgia was nearing the end of its C–141 production run and faced a bleak future. Unlike Boeing and Douglas, whose defense contracts were more or less balanced by commercial sales, Lockheed's dismal record in the commercial marketplace had left it almost completely dependent (more than 90 per cent of sales) on the Defense Department. With no other major military or civilian contracts in sight, Lockheed simply had to win the C–5A. Though Boeing and Douglas were in relatively better financial shape, they both felt the same way, because the C–5A promised to lead to future control of the commercial cargo aircraft market.

In April, 1965, the three companies submitted their final bids for the 115-plane contract: Boeing was high with a bid of $2.3 billion, Douglas was next with $2 billion, and Lockheed was a surprisingly low bidder with $1.9 billion. Since price is only one of many factors involved in the award of a major defense contract, however, the C–5A decision was still far from settled. Along with their bids the companies also dumped about 200,000 pages of supporting technical data on the Air Force — computerized projections of cost and construction schedules and aircraft performance. A 400-man C–5A Evaluation Group from the Air Force Systems Command pored over these papers for five months, during which time the companies were given the opportunity to modify their proposals. One of the main problems with the Lockheed design was that it did not meet the performance requirements for short takeoff and landing. Air Force officials discussed this deficiency with Lockheed executives, and the company worked up a new design with larger wings and flaps that supposedly solved the problem. Despite a significant increase in the size of its plane, however, Lockheed kept its cost estimate at $1.9 billion.

When all the modifications were in, the Evaluation Group presented its findings to an Air Force C–5A Source Selection Board, comprised of two major generals and two brigadier generals. After due deliberation, they rejected the Douglas bid on the grounds of inadequate design. Though Lockheed's enlarged design did meet the contract requirements, the board feared the design changes would cause schedule delays and cost increases (which turned out to be true). On the basis mainly of design superiority, the board finally picked Boeing's as the best proposal and sent its recommendation up to the top levels of the Air Force and DoD for the final decision.[4] (In competition with Pratt & Whitney, General Electric Company won the contract for the C-5A engine with a bid of $624 million.)

When word of the Source Selection Board's decision leaked out, as it usually does, Lockheed-Georgia, its employees, and much of Georgia reacted with shock. To Marietta, a half-hour's drive from Atlanta, and surrounding Cobb County, the C–5A contract and Lockheed-Georgia's financial health are matters of economic life or death. Take the company away and the region would revert to the boondocks that it was before Bell Aircraft built the plant there during the Second World War. When Bell stopped turning out B–29 bombers and shut the plant down in 1945, 32,000 people lost their jobs — a nightmare that many local citizens recalled vividly upon hearing that the C–5A contract might go to Boeing.

Lockheed took the plant over in 1951, and with the help of a continuing flow of orders from the Pentagon, plus $112 million worth of facilities built by the Air Force, the company brought prosperity back to Cobb County and grew into what is now the largest single industrial enterprise in the southeastern United States. "If it wasn't for Lockheed, Marietta wouldn't be where it's at," says Billy G. Petty, a Cobb County tax assessor. "The whole county would survive if Lockheed closed down, but it would cut the economy by fifty per cent."

No one had actually said Lockheed-Georgia would close down if it lost out on its bid for the C–5A, but the possibility was obvious. At the very least, such a loss would mean laying off 10,000 men upon the rapidly approaching end of production on the C–141 Starlifter. As though this weren't a big enough labor problem, the company also faced the threat of a strike by the plant's union, the International Association of Machinists, which represents most of the 1.3 million workers in the aerospace industry. A strike at this crucial point in the company's battle for the C–5A would have been disastrous, and Lockheed officials called in the union leaders to make this clear. "So we didn't have a strike," says C. A. Jenkins, Lockheed's industrial relations manager. "In that case the union showed quite a bit of fore-sight." [5] Since a strike might have ruined the company's chances for a contract which ultimately created another 10,000 jobs — and dues-paying members of the local IAM — the union's decision hardly required much foresight. (Once Lockheed had won the contract its labor relations returned to normal, and the company was plagued with a series of disputes and work stoppages, which of course helped to run up the cost of the C–5A.)

With its labor problems solved for the moment, Lockheed went to work in Washington, where it had the best friend a defense company could have — Georgia's late senator Richard Russell, then chairman of the Senate Armed Services Committee, chairman of the Senate Defense Appropriations subcommittee, and generally recognized as the most powerful member of the Senate. Over the years of Russell's power, Georgia changed from a relatively unindustrialized state into a major center of the defense industry, climbing from $117 million worth of prime defense contracts in 1960 to more than $1 billion annually today. In addition, the state bristles with five Air Force bases (one in Marietta), four Army bases, two naval air stations, and assorted other military depots, schools, and office buildings. The Defense Department's annual military and civilian payroll in Georgia amounts to nearly another billion dollars. Some of this was due to Russell's influence, but the services usually didn't need any hints from his office about where to establish a new base, particularly around the time the defense appropriations bill reached the Senate.

One of the first men to call upon the senator to talk about the C–5A was Marietta's mayor, Howard Atherton, who later said, "Without Russell we wouldn't have gotten the contract." One minor problem, however, as Mayor Atherton recalls, was that "Russell didn't think the C–5A was really needed." The senator had seen Air Force reports showing that the C–141 Starlifters, along with C-130 Hercules and other available transport planes, would be able to handle all military cargo needs for many years to come. Even Mayor Atherton now admits, "There's more porkbarrel than strategic need to the Galaxy. I never did think the plane was needed. Why the Starlifter can carry anything the C-5A can except a missile or some really big piece of Army gear. It was just a case that one C-5A could do the work of a couple of planes you already had flying." [6]

Whatever doubts Senator Russell had about the Pentagon's need for the C-5A, Mayor Atherton and Lockheed officials soon convinced him of Georgia's need for the C-5A contract. Though cynics might call this lobbying, it is far from the venal type that involves pressuring a congressman by means of money, votes, or other inducements into voting against his better judgment. In fact, a senator would be remiss in his duties as an elected representative if he did not use his influence to help his state win contracts — providing, of course, he is convinced that the contract is also in the best interest of the entire nation.

The question of lobbying and pressure may be irrelevant in this case, for no one who reaches Senator Russell's eminence on Capitol Hill needs much pressure when a $2 billion contract is at stake that could mean 20,000 jobs in his home state. The senator was soon arguing Lockheed-Georgia's case to his close friend at the White House, Lyndon Johnson. Since Russell's support was vital to the administration's legislative program (just as vital as Johnson's support had been to President Eisenhower), the President listened carefully. Of course he also listened carefully to Washington's Senator Henry Jackson (sometimes referred to on the Hill as "the Senator from Boeing") who pleaded the cause of the Seattle-based company.

Russell, however, obviously had far more clout. A few years later, President Johnson told an audience of Georgians gathered

around the first C–5A off the production line: "I would have you
good folks know there are a lot of Marietta, Georgia's, scattered
throughout our fifty states. All of them would like to have the
pride that comes from this production, but all of them don't have
the Georgia delegation." [7] To most knowledgeable people in
Georgia and back in the nation's capital, that meant only one
man — Russell.

Russell's role in the C–5A decision was the cause of some
amusement to those who recalled it a few years later when he led
the opposition to the Navy's proposed Fast Deployment Logistics
Ship (FDL), a gigantic transport whose function would be
strikingly similar to that of the C–5A. A fleet of FDL's would
give the U.S. a global network of floating military bases, each
able to disgorge at short notice a fully equipped combat division.
During the Senate debate on the FDL, Russell warned that they
would give "an impression that the U.S. has assumed the function
of policing the world, and can be thought to be at least considering intervention in any kind of strife or commotion occurring in
any nation of the world." The danger, according to Russell, was
that "if they can intervene, they will." [8] (Another strategic fault of
the FDL, which the senator did not mention, was that it would
be built in Mississippi.)

While the various political figures affected by the C–5A decision were busy doing what comes naturally to politicians, the
three companies seeking the contract were using whatever other
forms of influence they could bring to bear on the decision. For
Lockheed-Georgia, these ranged from briefings to military and
professional societies on the technical advances involved in their
C–5A design, to such crude ploys as hinting at plans for a new
sub-assembly plant in Charleston, South Carolina, home of
L. Mendel Rivers, then chairman of the House Armed Services
Committee.

As with most major defense contracts, much of the competition for the C–5A took place in the advertising pages of defense industry trade magazines and in slick briefings at conventions of such military-industrial organizations as the Air Force Association. The AFA's membership, along with industry executives, includes most top-ranking Air Force officers, particularly those involved in procurement. Realizing that its weak point was design, Lockheed-Georgia's briefings stressed the company's experience in building cargo aircraft and the excellence of its management. Lockheed PR men passed out handsome brochures at these meetings devoted to their C–5A management "team," with detailed organizational charts, photographs, and résumés.

It is difficult to measure the effect of all this pressure on the C–5A decision because there were so many other factors involved. The most important, according to Pentagon sources, was simply the desire to keep Lockheed-Georgia in business as a defense contractor. They point out that at that time Boeing had billions of dollars worth of commercial and other military orders on its books, and the loss of the C–5A contract, though painful, would not be a mortal blow. For Lockheed-Georgia, with no other major contracts, it might have been fatal.

To those who regularly follow the awards of major defense contracts this theory about the C–5A decision is quite plausible. In the last decade the Pentagon has somehow managed to spread its orders around fairly evenly among the big aerospace companies. (No one seems to worry about the smaller ones.) The result has been relative stability in an industry formerly plagued by cyclical booms and declines. In 1962, General Dynamics, which had been in serious financial trouble, got the billion-dollar TFX or F–111 jet fighter contract. Douglas won a $1.5 billion contract for the Air Force's Manned Orbiting Laboratory just after it became apparent that the company was out of the running for the C–5A. When the Defense Department finally picked Lockheed-Georgia to build the C–5A, Washington insiders figured that the next big contract, the supersonic transport (SST), would go to Boeing. It did.

For whatever reasons — and they may have included a few phone calls from the White House — Air Force Secretary Eugene Zuckert, USAF Chief of Staff General John P. McConnell, and other top Air Force officials overruled the experts on their own Source Selection Board and awarded the C–5A contract to Lockheed-Georgia. According to subsequent testimony before Congress, General McConnell cited the company's low bid as the decisive factor, claiming it represented "a substantial savings to the Government." [9] (The $400 million or so "saved" by this decision ultimately led to a cost overrun five times that figure.) Secretary Zuckert simply claimed the selection of Lockheed was "in the best interest of the Government," which could mean almost anything. [10]

The Pentagon did not immediately release the news of the C–5A decision because, according to tradition, the administration in power customarily allows friendly congressmen to announce awards of any sizable federal contract to companies in their states. While this might seem like a purely honorary gesture to some readers, it actually has considerable importance. First of all, an administration can forget to inform a recalcitrant congressman of such contract decisions, thereby not only depriving him of the honor of announcing it, but also giving him the appearance of an outsider among the Capitol's power brokers. To the average voter back home, the announcement implies that his congressman has somehow been instrumental in the decision. While this might be only vaguely true, the notion makes excellent fodder for the next campaign trail.

Another less savory advantage of making the first announcement is the option of calling a few friendly campaign contributors first, to let them in on the secret. Since the stock of the winner and losers generally react sharply to news of a major contract award, the value of such advance knowledge is obvious, and certainly worth remembering when the next campaign comes along. Of course congressmen publicly deny that they would pass along such timely stock tips to their friends, but knowledgeable Washington officials simply recognize this as a standard form of political patronage. Technically the announcements should not be made until the stock market has closed for the day, but somehow the word usually leaks out before then. (The tradition has continued under the Nixon administration, with the award of the $2 to 3 billion ASW anti-submarine aircraft to Lockheed, the $1.3 billion AMSA (B–1) strategic bomber to North American Rockwell, the $2 billion AWACS airborne radar system to Boeing, and the $2 billion DD–963 destroyer to Litton. In each case, the word got out well before the stock markets closed for the day.)

In accordance with custom, then, the Defense Department notified Senator Russell that Lockheed-Georgia had won the C–5A contract, and the senator broke the news to the company, the state of Georgia, and the press. (Meanwhile, the Secretary of the Air Force was explaining the decision in Senator Jackson's office to the assembled Washington state delegation.) At Marietta, workers yelled with joy when the word came over the plant's loudspeakers. Champagne corks popped all over northwestern Georgia that evening, from Aunt Fanny's Cabin in Marietta to the Playboy Club in Atlanta. Lockheed-Georgia immediately opened recruiting offices for engineers in Chicago, St. Louis (home of Douglas Aircraft), and New York. That fall Lockheed stock climbed from 50 to 60.

CHAPTER TWO

The Contract and Mr. Charles

"In my judgement, the C–5A award represents a major breakthrough in contracting techniques."

Robert McNamara,
Secretary of Defense

READERS WHO DISLIKE financial or legal details may skip this chapter, since it concerns the intricacies of the C–5A contract in particular, and defense contracting in general. Of course, you may also ignore the terms of the mortgage when you buy a home, the policy when you buy insurance, or the warranty when you buy a car. It's up to you. But at least with these items the decision to buy them is yours — you have a choice. With the C–5A you had none. The Air Force ordered the planes without consulting you, and whether you care about the contract or not, you are going to pay for them.

When the Air Force requested final proposals for the C–5A, it made a special point of informing the three bidding firms that "the target cost contained in the winning competitor's contract will remain firm . . . throughout the program." [1] While this may strike the layman as a needless caution, it actually represented a specific warning against "buying-in," a traditional defense industry practice in which a company deliberately submits an unreasonably low bid in order to win a contract, assuming that subsequent contract "change orders" (known as "contract nourishment") will boost the final price up to a healthy profit margin. There is considerable precedent for such an assumption. A 1962 study of 12 major weapon systems found that their final cost averaged 220 per cent above original quotations. A survey by the Brookings Institution of major DoD procurement contracts in the 1950s showed cost increases ranging from 100 to 700 per cent. "During the 1950's," the Brookings report concluded, "all large military contracts reflected an acceptance of contractor estimates which proved highly optimistic." [2] Despite official "concern" at the Pentagon, and numerous plans to cut down on this sort of thing, it still goes on. A 1969 check by the General Accounting Office on 38 major weapon programs currently underway found cost estimates already 50 per cent higher than the original contract figures — a total price increase of $20 billion.

When asked about these cost overruns, Pentagon and industry officials always have several standard explanations ready: inflation, labor troubles, subcontractor delays, "unforeseen technical difficulties," or "program changes" such as "increased sophistication" of design and improved performance. Whatever the explanation, the costs usually go up. If the generals and admirals still want the weapons — and they always do — the Defense Department has no choice but to keep on buying them from the same company regardless of cost.

The reason for this is that most large defense contracts are awarded on a "sole source" basis. The majority are negotiated with a single contractor; for the rest, several firms may compete at the research level, and even create prototypes, but the production contract generally goes to only one company. At that point the losing bidders generally disband their technical teams assembled for the bidding and research stages. By the time the winning contractor enters the production phase, given the increasing specialization of modern arms technology, it has become not only by contract, but also in fact, the sole possible source for the particular weapon. For at this point, no other company has the specific technical capability to produce it. In the slang of the defense industry, the winner is "locked-in" to the contract. From then on, the Pentagon must either pay the bill, even if it rises to two or three times the original price, or cancel the program, which would represent a tremendous waste of money. The Defense Department has occasionally canceled major contracts, but generally because the weapons simply did not work — not because the costs became too high.

Until the arrival of Robert McNamara as Secretary of Defense, few of the military and civilian officials around the Pentagon had ever worried much about whether a particular weapon was worth what they were paying for it. The question of worth just never seemed relevant in discussions of military technology and national security. Most generals have always felt that no price is too high to pay for the country's defense, particularly when it means a fancy new toy for their arsenal. (Their feelings must also be affected by the fact that unlike buyers in the commercial world, they are not spending their own money — but ours.) Besides, how does one measure the worth of a missile, in contrast to its price?

Secretary McNamara tried to answer this question by creating the Office of Systems Analysis and staffing it with a group of bright young civilians, many of them graduates of Harvard Business School, who became known around the Pentagon by the unflattering name, "the whiz kids." For the first time, under prodding from these "youngsters" only half their age, crusty generals and admirals who for years had based their requests for new weapons, ships, and planes almost completely on need, were forced to justify them in terms of something called "cost-effectiveness." In other words, the men from Systems Analysis were asking if the new weapons were the cheapest means of accomplishing the purposes for which they had been requested. The answer to this question of comparative cost-effectiveness required the use of complex computerized analysis — a language with which McNamara's whiz kids were familiar, but not the generals. So naturally, the generals wound up hating McNamara and the whiz kids and still blame them for nearly everything that has gone wrong with any weapon system since 1960.

However good or evil, Systems Analysis, as it functioned under McNamara, was mainly concerned with the initial decision-making process for a new weapon system and had little effect on the cost growth of programs once underway. This left the problem of "buy-ins" and spiraling costs unsolved. One of the men McNamara brought to the Pentagon to do something about this problem was Robert Charles, a former career employee of McDonnell Aircraft Corporation, and for seven years the company's executive vice-president. In 1963 Charles became Assistant Secretary of the Air Force for Installations and Logistics, one of the service's top administrative posts that included supervision of supply, maintenance, transportation, communications, and, most important, procurement. Charles later said he accepted the appointment "because I was convinced that we are spending more than we needed to on our national defense, that defense equipment was costing far too much, due to procurement methods which imposed little discipline, particularly competitive discipline, on either industry or Government, and that I could do something about it." [3]

Cynical readers may wonder about the wisdom of this appointment. They might reasonably feel that hiring a defense industry executive to supervise the government's defense contracts is like hiring a fox to guard the chicken coop. Anyone who is surprised by such a choice, however, obviously has little knowledge of

Pentagon personnel practices, for many of the civilian officials there in charge of research or procurement contracts have come from the same companies that get these contracts, and later return to them. Critics of this traffic pattern feel that it leads too easily to conflict-of-interest, but to those involved in it the passage back and forth between industry and DoD seems perfectly normal and reasonable. Their usual response to those who question it is, "Where the hell else do you expect us to find people who understand defense contracting?"

During the years that Mr. Charles was in charge of Air Force procurement, the service did a good deal of business with Mc-Donnell Aircraft. No one has ever suggested that Mr. Charles was instrumental in "swinging" any of this business to his former company, but some of those who worked with him at the Pentagon feel that his office was unusually generous in its dealings with all Air Force contractors. At a hearing in 1969 of the House Subcommittee on Military Operations, Gordon Rule, a high-ranking Navy procurement official, described Mr. Charles as a man who "believes no defense contractor should be allowed to lose money on a Government contract, and whose test of a contractor who has failed to live up to the terms of a contract is, 'Could any other contractor in that industry have done better?'" I strongly suggest that no man with such a philosophy should ever be appointed as Assistant Secretary for Installations and Logistics, because such a person provides the negotiators on the firing line the antithesis of sound procurement leadership." [4]

Anyone interested in Mr. Charles' procurement philosophy should read through a speech he gave on February 18, 1966, four months after the signing of the C–5A contract, to the Defense Industry Advisory Council, a group of two dozen chief executives of the largest DoD contractors, including Lockheed. The DIAC "helps" the Pentagon and the services formulate procurement policies. Charles told them that profits on many defense contracts were "too low," and that the industry was "over-controlled" by the government. Instead of DoD regulations, Mr. Charles proposed that "the self-policing constraints of competition" were sufficient to guarantee reasonable profit levels.[5] One can safely assume the defense industry executives of the DIAC found these words comforting, coming from the Air Force's top procurement official.

Robert Charles' major contribution to defense procurement during his years in public office was the creation of a new method of contracting called the "Total Package Procurement" concept (TPP), which was first used on the C–5A. Since TPP had never been tried before, many Defense officials privately wondered how effective it would be. Defense Secretary McNamara, however, called the C–5A award "a damned good contract" and told Congress, it "represents a major breakthrough in contracting techniques."

On paper it did. Until then, competing firms (when there was competition) bid only for an initial research and development contract. Although R & D generally represents only about 20 per cent of the total cost of a weapon system, the winner of this contract could feel assured of receiving the follow-on contract for actual production. Having already invested millions of dollars for R & D, the Defense Department was almost forced to accept the company's bid for the production contract because the complexity of the research generally made it impossible to switch to another contractor at this point. This meant that each time the Defense Department awarded an R & D contract it was essentially buying a pig-in-a-poke, with little control over 80 per cent of the final cost of the program.

Charles called this "iceberg procurement" and designed his new system of contracting to give the government as much control as possible over the entire acquisition process — hence the name Total Package Procurement. Under TPP competing firms submit proposals covering research, development, *and* production, including performance and delivery commitments. In theory, at least, this would prevent excessive charges by a sole source contractor who had "locked-in" with just the R & D contract.

The very completeness of the new Total Package contract has turned out to be one of its biggest problems, for the entire procurement process on a major program can easily stretch out over a period of five to ten years. The C-5A contract, for example, meant that the Air Force and Lockheed were negotiating in 1965 on the basis of cost estimates for work that would not be completed until 1972. All sorts of things can happen in the space of seven years, and in the case of the C-5A, most of them have.

Awkward as it is, the old two-stage method of contracting has certain advantages over TPP. On many contracts research and development leads to the construction of a prototype which can be examined and tested before the signing of a production contract. This "fly before you buy" concept allows for the inclusion of design changes that often cannot be foreseen before this stage. Even in programs where the construction of a prototype is impractical because of size and cost, the experience gained through the R & D stage gives the contractor and the Defense Department a much better basis on which to estimate the cost of production. Also, by having the opportunity to draw up the final contract some years after the program is first conceived, the services can more accurately judge their strategic and logistical needs.

The C-5A contract included everything but weather conditions: research, development, testing, and evaluation on five experimental planes; an initial production run of 53 planes (Run A); an optional second run of 57 more planes (Run B); flight and ground test programs; crew and maintenance training for six squadrons; ground support equipment and spare parts. In addition, Assistant Secretary Charles wrote several provisions into the contract designed to prevent the most common abuses in defense procurement. Schedule delays would bring penalties of $12,000 per day for each of the first 16 planes delivered late (with a maximum penalty of $11 million). The contractor would have to absorb the costs of correcting any structural deficiencies and would earn no profit on costs incurred as a result of design changes. The contractor would have to guarantee delivery of a plane that would meet extremely detailed performance specifications.

In the modest opinion of its author, the final document was "probably the toughest contract for a major defense system ever entered into by the Pentagon." Whatever one thinks of the contract, Mr. Charles should be complimented for his foresight in including all those special provisions, for nearly every one of the problems they were designed to prevent ultimately occurred, despite the provisions. And "tough" as the contract supposedly is, the Air Force has not always tried to force Lockheed to live up to it.

In terms of price and profit, the C–5A contract utilized what is known in the trade as "fixed price incentive." This means the contractor's price is fixed in the contract with a specific margin of profit — 10 per cent in the case of the C–5A. Thus Lockheed's bid of $1.945 billion represented an actual "target" cost of $1.769 billion plus a profit of about $177 million. As an "incentive" to hold costs down, the contract gives the company an opportunity to increase its profit by producing the plane for less than the target cost (which almost never happens) and penalizes him by reducing the profit if costs rise above the target. This threat is offset, however, in the C–5A contract by another clause, which requires the government to pay 70 per cent of costs above the target price up to a "ceiling" price set at 130 per cent of the target.

If costs run above the ceiling price, the C–5A contract is

governed by its most ingenious and controversial clause, "the repricing formula," referred to by its critics as "the golden handshake," or the "sweetheart clause." According to *Fortune* magazine, the repricing formula "was worked out by a computer, and virtually requires a computer to understand." [6] Basically it uses the cost experience on the 53 planes in production Run A as a basis for renegotiating the cost of the 57 planes in Run B. If costs on Run A rise above the ceiling price (which itself is 30 per cent over the target price) the over-ceiling percentage is multiplied by a factor of 1.5, or 2 if costs go higher than 140 per cent of the target. The resulting figure is then used to multiply the original target cost of Run B, producing new, higher target and ceiling prices for Run B. Simple? (If the repricing formula seems confusing, the reader may be reassured to know that Congress, the General Accounting Office, the Air Force, and Lockheed have also found it confusing.)

Mr. Charles claimed the purpose of the repricing formula is to prevent "catastrophic losses" on the part of the contractor, yet when asked by Senator Proxmire to cite examples of companies losing money on major defense contracts, Charles could not recall any.[7] Critics claim the formula acts as a reverse incentive, rewarding an inefficient contractor by enabling him to make up any losses on Run A by getting a higher price on Run B. It might even encourage him to purposely pad costs on Run A as a means of increasing his profit on the total contract. For example, if costs of Run A rise merely 35 per cent higher than expected, or 5 per cent above ceiling, it would result in a very slight rise in the cost of the planes in Run B. But if the cost overrun on Run A were to reach 100 per cent — which it has — then all the multiplication and factors and percentages would mean that the Air Force would end up paying 240 per cent of the contract price for Run B. A former DoD official who served during the time of the

C–5A award recalls, "When I heard about this repricing clause, I could see right away there would be trouble." There was.

Nearly everyone outside the Air Force and Lockheed now agrees that much of the trouble with the C–5A program was due to a deliberate buy-in by Lockheed. When Air Force officials opened the three bids, they were astonished by Lockheed's price of only $1.9 billion, particularly since that company's design called for a larger and heavier plane than those of Boeing or Douglas. The Air Force's own internal estimate for that contract had been $2.2 billion. Boeing executives later admitted that even their bid of $2.3 billion was a trifle "optimistic," for they had figured they had only a 30 per cent chance of fulfilling the contract at that price. According to their calculations, the cost would probably come closer to $2.5 billion, and might run as high as $2.9 billion. Even *Air Force* magazine, an aerospace industry trade publication, referred discreetly to Lockheed's bid as "rather low."

Years later, Air Force officials told Congress they had detected "a degree of optimism" in the Lockheed bid. Even Robert Charles, who had supposedly designed the contract to prevent this sort of thing, later admitted that "practically everyone thought that the bid was lower than the actual costs would be. But you can't be sure of this. When you have responsible companies like Lockheed, Boeing, and Douglas bidding, what do you do? Do you go back and say, 'Your price is too low'? I don't think so. They're big boys." [8]

Most people in the aerospace industry feel that despite the supposed restrictions of Mr. Charles' contract, Lockheed was probably counting on later design changes and the repricing formula to raise the price well beyond that of the contract, making their low bid a successful gamble. Even Charles himself recognized this possibility: "They may have believed we wouldn't hold them

28 THE C–5A SCANDAL

to the contract. And there would be some merit in such belief. After all, we hadn't in the past."

Probably the main reason for Lockheed's buy-in on the C–5A is the fact that the company simply had to have the contract to stay in business. An investigation five years later by the Securities and Exchange Commission produced evidence that Lockheed knew its bid was too low. The SEC report reveals Lockheed's top management ordered the staff cost proposals cut by 10 per cent, in order to win the contract.[9] According to the SEC report, an Air Force cost analyst attached to the program told Lockheed, in the summer of 1965, its cost estimates on the C–5A were *much too low.*[10]

Lockheed officials still deny that they bought in on the C–5A and insist their bid was realistic. As Daniel J. Haughton, chairman of the board at Lockheed, later told a congressional committee: "I sincerely felt we could design and build the airplane at the price we quoted."[11] If one accepts Mr. Haughton's sincerity, one can only conclude that he and his colleagues made an astounding error in judgment in their C–5A bid — as astounding as that of the Air Force officials who accepted it.

CHAPTER THREE

Construction, Confusion and Concealment

"We are experiencing difficulty in obtaining adequate visibility into causes of these indicated problems."

Leonard Marks,
Assistant Secretary of the Air Force
for Financial Management

THOUGH THE PUBLIC and Congress did not learn about the technical and cost problems on the C–5A until November, 1968, troubles actually began shortly after Lockheed started work on the plane in the fall of 1965. Early in 1966 the men down at Marietta began to encounter a series of unforeseen technical problems referred to in the trade as "unk-unks" — or unknown unknowns. Wind tunnel tests on models of the Lockheed design showed too much drag for short takeoffs, which required the redesign of the wings, nose, and other parts. In addition to the drag problem, Lockheed engineers discovered that their revised, larger design would exceed the contract's weight requirements. They managed to cut the weight by using lighter but more expensive metals in construction, such as titanium fasteners for the body sections. There were other problems which, though less technical, were equally bothersome. Many of them were caused by the sheer size of the plane and led harried Lockheed executives to refer to its construction in terms normally used in shipbuilding. For example, the 63-foot-high tail sections were too big for the largest assembly buildings at Marietta and had to be fastened to the fuselage in specially built facilities.

Today, Lockheed officials claim most of these technical problems were the natural result of work that advanced the "state-of-the-art," a common phrase in defense contracting referring to the frontiers of technology. According to Pentagon statements during the contracting process, however, the Total Package Procurement concept was first applied to the C–5A contract specifically because the Air Force foresaw no development or construction problems that would require any breakthoughs in aerospace technology. In other words, the Air Force felt the C–5A would not involve an "advance in the state-of-the-art."

This apparent contradiction over state-of-the-art represents another time-honored tradition in defense contracting. When the companies make their bids, and when the Defense Department requests funds from Congress, there is rarely any talk about state-of-the-art. The competing firms are eager to convince the services that they already have the technological capability to build the particular weapon, and DoD officials, in turn, are eager to assure Congress that the weapon can easily be built for what they are asking. Once the contract is signed, however, and Congress authorizes the funds, the formerly simple weapon often acquires an awesome complexity, forcing the company's engineers to "break through" the frontiers of technology. As costs begin to rise, the magic phrase is heard. The company tells the Pentagon and the Pentagon tells Congress that the reason for the cost increase is that the contract requires an "advance in the state-of-the-art." This generally explains the cost increase to everyone's satisfaction.

Despite Lockheed's efforts to overcome their technological problems, Air Force plant representatives were sufficiently concerned about them to send the company a warning in December, 1966. Receiving no reply, the Air Force issued a "cure notice," on February 1, 1967, stating that unless the technical deficiencies were soon solved, the contract might be "terminated" for default.

This cure notice was no mere slap on the wrist. In fact this was the first time the Air Force had ever issued one on a major contract, despite what many critics of defense spending would feel were numerous other equally or even more appropriate occasions.

In order to solve the design engineering problems quickly (the contract called for stiff financial penalties for schedule delays), Lockheed had to expand the scope of its development program. This occurred at a time when the growing U.S. involvement in Vietnam was causing a boom in the military aircraft industry, which in turn caused a shortage of aeronautical engineers. Lockheed was forced to pay its own men for a great deal of overtime, hire extra men at higher wages, and farm some of its work out to engineering firms in England. At one time as many as 850 British engineers were working on the C–5A, causing more problems with differing techniques and overseas liaison.

Faced with these mounting costs for engineering, Lockheed tried repeatedly to get the Air Force C–5 System Program Office to relax some contract specifications. An SPO memo tells how Lockheed also tried to "maneuver within the contract framework to get the Air Force to pay for work we contend is already on contract." [1] The SPO refused to budge, however, which must have come as a rude shock to Lockheed. In the past, whenever such problems had developed on its military programs, Lockheed could always count on the Air Force to waive certain difficult contract requirements, or at least issue enough change orders to allow the company to recover any "unexpected expenses" involved in meeting the requirements. In the Lockheed Annual Report for 1969, one can sense a tone of petulant surprise at the Air Force's attempt to make the company live up to its contract:

> The government also demanded rigid adherence to contractual performance specifications and delivery dates. These demands, although understandable, resulted in expenditures by contractor far

beyond the original estimates . . . Contract terms were regarded as sacrosanct, even though a relaxation of specifications and delivery dates could have greatly lessened costs.[2]

Forced to live up to its contract at this point, Lockheed had to spend millions of extra dollars — money not planned for in the company's original cost estimates. The extra costs began showing up as increased overhead on Lockheed's monthly program reports to the Air Force early in 1966, but Lockheed solved this problem by means of an ingenious though standard defense industry practice. Claiming their initial budget estimates had been mistaken, they merely increased the budget for this development stage, and the overruns disappeared. Nearly everyone in the Air Force accepted this procedure.

One of the few who didn't was Ernest Fitzgerald, a civilian cost expert who held the post of Deputy for Management Systems in the Office of the Assistant Secretary of the Air Force for Financial Management. Since the C–5A was then the largest Air Force contract, Fitzgerald spent a good deal of his time following the plane's financial progress. He was also a member of a special C–5A steering committee charged with keeping track of the plane's development.

In January, 1966, Fitzgerald made a routine visit to Marietta along with other Air Force officers connected with the C–5A program. In discussions with Lockheed officials they learned that overhead rates for the program were well above those estimated in the contract. In his report, Fitzgerald wrote: "If not offset by underruns elsewhere, the overhead increases represent an incipient C–5A overrun." [3] This incident is worth noting, for it was the first mention of an overrun on the C–5A. Though it continued to grow steadily from this point on, the Air Force did not admit the fact publicly until nearly three years later, and only then because Fitzgerald broke the news to Congress.

This early report appeared in the Office of Financial Management's Weekly Staff Digest Report that goes to all top USAF officials. It even came to the attention of the new Secretary of the Air Force, Harold Brown, who asked an assistant: "The overhead rates are Lockheed's problem, aren't they? Can they increase the price beyond the ceiling? I don't think so." Brown's assistant, an Air Force colonel, agreed. "You are correct in your statement that Lockheed cannot increase our price of the current C–5A contract beyond the ceiling price — providing we introduce no changes to that contract." [4]

Brown and his assistant were both wrong. Not only did the Air Force later introduce hundreds of changes in the contract that allowed Lockheed to raise the price, but the company managed to pass along the extra overhead costs as well. Brown was strangely unaware of the controversial "repricing formula," by which the cost of any overruns (including overhead) on the first 53 planes in production Run A would be figured into and thus raise the price of the 57 aircraft in Run B. Though Brown was undoubtedly busy at the time, he was also Secretary of the Air Force. As such, one might expect him to have a better knowledge of the Air Force's largest and most controversial contract, awarded only four months before.

During the summer and fall of 1966, engineering man-hours should have begun to taper off as the plane moved from development toward production. They didn't, and the C–5A reports from Marietta began to show substantial overruns. In August, Lockheed had spent $45 million for design work that had a planned cost of $35 million. By October the engineering overrun was up to $18 million, and still growing. Lockheed solved the problem on paper by merely increasing its budget for this period, and the November report showed costs "back on target."

Fitzgerald had been following the growing overrun, however, and was sufficiently concerned about it to bring the matter up with Robert Charles. After their conversation Charles called the

Air Force's C–5 System Program director, Colonel Guy Townsend, who then called Fitzgerald and accused him of "conveying
unsubstantiated information to Mr. Charles." He told Fitzgerald
that the engineering changes were too complicated to discuss at
this point and wondered why he was concerned with them. Fitzgerald replied that the engineering changes were largely responsible for the C–5A overrun thus far. This chat ended with Colonel
Townsend insisting that engineering was none of Fitzgerald's business and that he sould leave it to the C–5 System Program Office.[5]

The reason I call this early dispute to the reader's attention is
that it represents a conflict which pervades both the C–5A story
and all defense contracting. High-ranking officers of uniformed
services are extremely jealous of any interference in their affairs
by Pentagon civilians, and Fitzgerald, a civilian, was interfering.
The immediate responsibility for each weapon under contract
rests with a System Program Office, staffed by uniformed officers
for whom the weapon becomes a vital part of their careers. Anyone — particularly a civilian outsider — who points out problems
in the weapon's development is thereby raising questions about
their management of it. Anyone who questions their management
ability is endangering their careers.

The main concern of most procurement and System Program
officers is to keep the program flowing. The weapon should work
and be delivered on schedule. If costs end up double the original
estimates, that's of little concern, for these officers will usually
have been transferred long before the final bill comes in. In
this way, they unfortunately become true partners of the company
whose work they supposedly supervise, since their goals are the
same: keep the program running smoothly, don't rock the boat,
and never mind the cost. As a result of this partnership of shared
concerns, the Defense Department loses effective control over
these men, and the public loses their protection of its investment.

When men like Fitzgerald try to keep accurate track of costs, Pentagon procurement officials and the company often draw together in a united front against them. In the case of the C–5A, however, there was no way to keep the rising costs from showing up occasionally on paper, and Fitzgerald spotted them. In November, 1966, he and other members of a high-level C–5A cost control team from the Pentagon made a trip down to Georgia to inquire about the overrun. Lockheed officials there denied there was one, but refused to supply any figures. Fitzgerald turned in a report upon his return that led his boss, Assistant Secretary Leonard Marks, to warn the Air Force Comptroller of "significant incipient cost problems on the Lockheed C–5A contract." In the euphemistic language of Pentagon memos, Marks wrote: "We are experiencing difficulty in obtaining adequate visibility into causes of these indicated problems. . . . It appears that Lockheed is holding back full disclosure of the information generated by their own systems." [6] In English, this means Lockheed was trying to cover up the C–5A cost overrun.

Three weeks later, in December, 1966, the team of Air Force cost analysts made another trip to Lockheed-Georgia and found that the overrun had reached $212 million, caused mainly by engineering man-hours and overhead. One member of this team, Colonel Larry Killpack, chief of the Air Force Cost and Economic Information Bureau, sent a report to Major General Harry Goldsworthy, head of the Air Force Systems Command's Aeronautical Systems Division, warning him: "My quick analysis of the situation is that Lockheed is in serious difficulty on the C–5A." [7] Another team member, Colonel Joe Warren, a cost efficiency expert from the Office of Financial Management, wrote this report to Assistant Secretary Marks:

> The second briefing was very much like seeing the rerun of an old movie. The plot still has drama and suspense, the script was excellent, the acting superb, but the outcome will be the same as it

was the first, second or tenth time it was shown. The contract
costs will be exceeded . . . The coming cost increases will be
more than justified, supported, rationalized and explained by the
contractor. His position will be supported by the Air Force.[8]

Naturally, both Lockheed and the Air Force C-5 System
Program Office found such reports embarrassing, and complained
to USAF headquarters about these visits by Pentagon cost analysts. Rather than doing anything about the cost overrun, the
Air Force took action against its cost analysts, the way emperors
in ancient times ordered messengers bearing unpleasant news put
to death. Colonel Killpack was transferred to Vietnam, and
Colonel Warren suddenly acquired unique qualifications to become Air Attaché in Addis Ababa, Ethiopia. Orders were cut
for sending him there, but his friends at USAF headquarters
managed to block the move. He was still taken off the C-5A
program, however, and transferred to a computer manager job
in the Pentagon.

Even at Lockheed-Georgia, some officials were concerned
about the progress of the C-5A program. Jack Tooley, a former
Army airlift expert who was working as a civilian adviser to
Lockheed, found incredible inefficiency on the production line.
"From time to time," he recalled later, "since I had nothing better
to do, I would walk through the main plant, observing what was
going on. The number of workers loafing on the job was absolutely unbelievable. In fact, my major contributions to Lockheed
probably were these trips through the production line, since
workers seeing me without a badge, and in a suit and white shirt,
went back to work, as they were not sure of who I was." Tooley
talked to one supervisor who admitted he had 40 more men in
his department than he needed. Tooley also found men making
ten dollars an hour who were "not doing anything, and yet spent
60 hours a week doing it because that is what the contract called

for." [9] Unable to take much of this, Tooley finally quit in disgust.

From this point on, the history of the C–5A's cost growth begins to sound like a military version of *Alice in Wonderland*. Critics who have accused Defense officials of being ignorant of cost overruns generally are not giving them enough credit. In the case of the C–5A, at least, the highest Air Force authorities were both aware of and concerned about the overruns — so concerned in fact that they managed to make them disappear.

Near the end of 1966, the Comptroller of the Defense Department requested a cost summary on the C–5A from the Air Force. The report he received in January, 1967, showed no overrun at all, made no mention of Lockheed's $212 million "budget increase," and failed to supply most of the data requested. Since the overrun was by then common knowledge throughout the upper levels of the Pentagon, and since the report was incomplete and blatantly misleading, the Comptroller's office sent it back to the Air Force for "reaccomplishment." In a memo accompanying the request for resubmission, Leonard Marks specifically instructed the Air Force Systems Command to include a discussion of the overrun, pointing out carefully that "This increase is known to OSD" [10] (Office of the Secretary of Defense).

When he learned that the $212 million overrun report was going to appear in a January, 1967, management summary, Lieutenant General Duward Crow, then Comptroller of the Air Force Systems Command (and now Comptroller of the Air Force), had the report deleted on the grounds that the figures had not been "reviewed" by proper Air Force authorities.[11] This review took a great deal of time and involved several further cost studies. For nearly two more years, Lockheed's C–5A cost overrun continued to grow. Though reports of this growth regularly reached the highest Air Force authorities, no word of it appeared in either the Systems Command's monthly contract summary reports or the Air Staff's cost performance reports.

Those close to the C–5A program, however, were well aware of the growing cost problems. In January, 1967, Lockheed requested $79 million in additional funding[12] — a 57 per cent increase over the initial request for that year. Confronted with this increase, a high-ranking Air Force official told a February meeting of Pentagon officials assigned to supervise the C–5A: "This is the first major aircraft system to begin operational system development after completing an extended contract definition phase. The central idea of contract definition is to define achievable performance and to develop realistic schedules and credible cost estimates in relation thereto. Clearly Lockheed flunks the course on this basis." [13]

By the summer of 1967, the C–5A's cost problems caused the Air Force to dispatch a special study group to examine the program. Among the conclusions of this study group was the statement that Lockheed's earlier budgets submitted to the Air Force were "so unrealistic one wonders if they were developed for government consumption." [14]

On November 15, 1967, Air Force Chief of Staff General John McConnell reported to Secretary of Defense McNamara: "We have been quite successful in controlling cost growth in the C–5A program as a result of changes." He admitted a Lockheed "cost growth" of $240 million, but claimed that current estimates for completion were still below the Air Force spring 1965 estimate. Nine days later, however, McNamara received a sharply contrasting memo from his civilian DoD Comptroller, Robert Anthony, a former Harvard Business School professor of accounting who had brought his own team of cost analysts to the Pentagon. General McConnell, according to Anthony, was mistaken. Instead of a $240 million "cost growth," Anthony claimed that the Air Force's own figure for the C–5A overrun was actually $351 million, and growing higher. Instead of a completion cost estimate below the original, the current USAF estimate, said Anthony, was nearly $500 million above it.[15]

Confronted with these gross errors in General McConnell's report, one can conclude either that he made a remarkable mistake, that he deliberately concealed the C–5A overrun from the Secretary of Defense, or that the Air Force had failed to inform its own Chief of Staff about one of the largest cost increases in the history of military procurement. One other possible explanation, of course, is that the Air Force's own figures on the C–5A may have been so confused that they actually had no accurate estimates. Looking back on this period, Anthony recalls, "The first information we got from the Air Force on the C–5A was so unintelligible we couldn't make any sense out of it." [16]

In February, 1968, Lockheed submitted a year-end report to the Air Force, showing no series cost problems. When the Air Force's C–5 System Program Office analyzed the data in this report, however, it came up with an estimate that showed Lockheed with a potential loss of $316 million. Lockheed claimed the SPO estimates were far too high and complained about them to USAF headquarters. SPO then sent another cost study team to Lockheed-Georgia that spent a few weeks making a full-scale analysis of the C–5A program. When this group came up with figures even higher than the previous estimates, Lockheed protested again.[17] One reason Lockheed was so concerned about these overrun estimates is that the Air Force was approaching a decision on whether to order the additional planes of Run B. A later investigation pointed out that "it was definitely in Lockheed's favor to keep the Air Force in the dark on the cost of Run A because of the upcoming Run B decision." [18]

In March, 1968, when the Assistant Secretary of the Air Force

for Research and Development, Alexander Flax, was asked by
the House Subcommittee on Defense Appropriations about the
C-5A's cost, he replied that the current estimates were still
"within the range" of the original target and ceiling costs.[19] General Crow added that the Air Force expected no serious price
problems with the C-5A: "As a matter of fact, the cost history
of this program is probably the best cost history we have ever had
on any program." [20] (When confronted with these embarrassing
testimonials a year later, after the $2 billion overrun had been
exposed, Air Force officials told Congress they only learned of
the C-5A overrun in April, 1968, *just* after making those statements before the Defense Appropriations Subcommittee.) During
the spring of 1968 the USAF Systems Command conducted a
"cost review" of the C-5A program, which showed an overrun of
$570 million, but still no one informed Congress. The overrun
was covered up with another "program change" which increased
Lockheed's budget requirements by $570 million above earlier
estimates. Again, the overrun had disappeared.

By the summer of 1968, Fitzgerald had become so concerned
at the absence of any official reference to the C-5A overrun — by
then, he estimated, more than $1 billion — that he requested au-
dit assistance from Anthony's office. The auditors encountered
considerable difficulty, however, in obtaining any information on
the C-5A from the Air Force Systems Command, or the C-5 System Program Office. All they were told was that the overrun information had been deleted from their reports "per direction of
higher headquarters." Faced with the Air Force's lack of cooperation, they were unable to complete their audit.[21]

When a General Accounting Office audit finally pinned them
down, System Program officers confirmed the inaccuracy of their
reports and said they had received orders from Assistant Secretary
Charles to the effect that "the anticipated overrun on the C-5A

program should not be reflected in routine management type reports." [22] Charles later explained this action to the House Armed Services Committee on the grounds that cost experience on the C–5A at that time was still insufficient to justify a formal overrun report. Instead, he ordered still another "careful and detailed study," which took six months more, and found the over-run had grown to nearly $1 billion.[23]

By means of such cost reviews, program changes, and other budget "modifications," the Air Force successfully managed to keep the C–5A's cost overrun at least quiet, if not a complete secret. Meanwhile, Lockheed's PR men were grinding out press releases hailing the completion of each step in the plane's development. At industry trade meetings and Air Force gatherings they passed out slick C–5A brochures with excellent color photographs. Whenever high-ranking Air Force generals flew into Marietta to inspect the plane's progress, Lockheed-Georgia executives gave them red carpet receptions and impressive briefings.

The high point in this publicity build-up came on Saturday, March 2, 1968, at the "roll-out" ceremony for the first completed C–5A — an occasion similar to the formal launching of a ship. The roll-out of any new military plane is always an occasion for ceremony and speeches by company and Defense officials, but the C–5A was no ordinary plane. Using nearby Dobbins Air Force Base, a flock of Air Force jets flew in — at taxpayers' expense — with USAF Secretary Harold Brown; Chief of Staff John McConnell; members of the House and Senate Armed Services Committees; and hundreds of other government and military dignitaries. To the dozens of reporters from defense industry journals and the Pentagon press corps, Lockheed PR men passed out bulky C–5A press kits which proclaimed the plane was meeting all cost and production schedules.

Up on the official platform, before a crowd of 40,000 Lockheed workers and other citizens of Georgia, Governor Lester
Maddox welcomed the day's guest of honor, Lyndon Johnson.
In a dedicatory speech obviously aimed at a nation in turmoil
over its role in the Vietnam war, the President declared that the
C-5A "opens a new era in America's power." "For the first
time," he said, "our fighting men will be able to travel with their
equipment to any spot on the globe where we might be forced to
stand — rapidly and more efficiently than ever . . . We are observing a long leap forward in the effective military might of
America . . . The aircraft that we roll out here today is the
signal that we shall not abandon the road of responsibility. We
shall march it proudly." [24]

The crowd at Marietta that day cheered these words, and the
President and his family flew happily on to Ramey Air Force
Base in Puerto Rico for a vacation. Some of those who read the
speech later, however, were troubled. Fearing the C-5A would
somehow lead to additional military entanglements in faraway
places, they thought Mr. Johnson's speech sounded distinctly like
the rattling of sabers.

General Howell Estes, who directs the Military Airlift Command which will operate the C-5As, told the audience that combined with the C-141 Starlifter, the new transport would "provide
the U.S. with a strategic deployment capability second to none
in the world." General James Ferguson, chief of the Air Force
Systems Command, which supervised the C-5A's development,
claimed it would have a "revolutionary" impact on strategic
airlift and pointed out that its operating costs would be "competitive" with that of ships. He did not mention the cost of the
plane itself. [25]

Thanks to the diligence of Lockheed's publicity staff, press
accounts of the roll-out ceremony referred to the C-5A as a "$20
million aircraft," although both Lockheed and Air Force officials

close to the program already knew the planes would most likely end up costing at least double that figure. Taking their cue from the Lockheed statements in their C–5A press kits, most reporters filed stories describing the plane's marvelous capabilities as though they had already been demonstrated, when actually the Galaxy had not yet flown. Not everyone at Marietta that day, however, was so confident. One young Lockheed-Georgia mechanic who had worked on the C–5A stared balefully at the huge plane as it was towed out of its hangar and muttered, "It'll never get off the ground." [26]

It did do that. Nearly five months later, in June, as the strains of "Dixie" came from a cockpit tape recorder, the first C–5A lumbered down the runway at Marietta and rose slowly into the early morning haze. "While the technological world held its collective breath," gushed *Air Force* magazine, the C–5A climbed to 10,000 feet and performed several simple test maneuvers over a thinly populated section of northeast Georgia. "It flew beautifully," exclaimed Lockheed-Georgia's chief test pilot, Leo Sullivan, after landing. "It couldn't have been nicer." [27] Sullivan got the rest of the day off and was honored the following week by his hometown, Pomona, California, with a "Leo Sullivan Day."

Sullivan told aerospace reporters the C–5A handled as easily as the much smaller C–141, although he admitted that because of the sophisticated flight simulators on which he had practiced, and on which all C–5A pilots will be weaned, "There aren't many surprises for the test pilot anymore." A similar wistfulness is expressed by a story that circulated among pilots when the giant transport was first conceived. According to this tale, the C–5A's cockpit, in addition to its many dials, buttons, lights, and computers, would have a glassed-in compartment containing a smiling, confident-looking pilot. On the glass would be this sign: "Break Only in Case of Emergency."

CHAPTER FOUR

Options

"The person to protect is the American taxpayer. We deserve to be protected, not Lockheed."

Representative Martha Griffiths

ALTHOUGH THE AIR FORCE has always insisted that everyone with a "need to know" knew about the C–5A cost overrun, those with such a need were limited to just a few high Air Force officials. Somehow, no one at USAF headquarters felt Congress or the public had a need or right to know about the cost of the C–5A. When the USAF Aeronautical Systems Division Commander, General Harry Goldsworthy, was asked before the House Military Operations Subcommittee why the Air Force never got around to telling Congress about it, he gave this typical bureaucratic non-answer: "Well, we devoted a great amount of discussion and thought as to how we would address the issue. There were many proposals which were reviewed at that time with, particularly Secretary Charles, and they involved, in the summer of 1968, quite an extensive study effort in this direction. As far as notification to Congressional authorities, I do not know, I have nothing on that." [1]

The man who finally informed Congress about the C–5A cost overrun was Ernest Fitzgerald. During his long struggle to get the Air Force to control costs on the C–5A and other programs, he had acquired a reputation for being stubborn and outspoken.

In the fall of 1968, word of Fitzgerald's reputation reached the staff of Senator William Proxmire's Subcommittee on Economy in Government, which was planning hearings on military procurement. The subcommittee contacted Fitzgerald and asked if he would be willing to testify about problems of military procurement. Fitzgerald agreed, but his superiors attempted to prevent his appearance before the subcommitee. Proxmire persisted, however, and finally succeeded.

On November 13, 1968, Fitzgerald testified that on the basis of the Air Force's own current figures, the projected overrun for the total C–5A program would probably reach at least $2 billion, and that Lockheed would run more than 100 per cent over its target price. Asked how this overrun had come about, Fitzgerald offered three reasons: initial underestimation of costs, ineffective cost controls, and what he termed "corporate strategy," referring to the reverse incentive of the contract's repricing formula.[2] Although the Air Force immediately issued a press release denying the $2 billion estimate, and putting the figure closer to $1 billion, the disclosure made front page headlines across the country. Proxmire blasted the Air Force for concealing the cost increase from Congress and asked the General Accounting Office to investigate the entire C–5A program.

For an institution that can be infuriatingly slow and cumbersome at times, the Defense Department can also act with remarkable dispatch when speed seems vital to its own security. While this may be true for any bureaucratic organization, the Pentagon has a particular flair for frustrating its critics with delaying tactics and startling them with surprise attacks. In response to the public exposure of the C–5A cost overrun, the Pentagon gave a brilliant demonstration of its competence in such bureaucratic guerrilla warfare.

First it had to deal with the General Accounting Office investi-

gation called for by Senator Proxmire. The GAO serves Congress
as an auditor of federal spending, and its investigations, while
conducted with varying degrees of diligence, have at least the
power of congressional authority. In the case of the C-5A, however, in which the GAO depended on the cooperation of the
Pentagon, that authority had very little effect.[3]

When the GAO first requested cost data on the plane, the Air
Force simply refused, claiming the material was "classified," or
secret. In the past, the Defense Department used to classify
material because its release might endanger the nation's security.
Over the years, however, this phrase has acquired an increasingly
broad and vague meaning, and today DoD routinely classifies a
great deal of information that has no conceivable relation to national security. With the rise of congressional and journalistic
criticism of defense spending in recent years, the Pentagon has
begun to classify almost any information that could prove embarrassing. (While all federal departments and agencies naturally
try to prevent damaging publicity, the others, lacking the power
to classify, are forced to resort to more difficult and less blatant
subterfuges.) The result has been that as the public's curiosity
about defense spending has increased, its ability to acquire any
useful information on the subject has diminished.

The Air Force tried to explain its classification of the C-5A
cost data on the grounds that its release might "compromise" the
negotiations then underway with Lockheed for the price of the 57
planes in production Run B. The USAF official who used the
word "compromise" obviously meant that the government's position in the negotiations would be damaged if its estimates for
Run A — which already differed considerably from Lockheed's
— were made public. Those who have carefully followed the
history of the C-5A, however, feel that another unintended sense
of "compromise" more accurately describes the Air Force's re-

luctance to release its cost estimates: "to make liable to danger, suspicion, scandal, etc., to damage the reputation of." What makes the latter definition more plausible is the fact that at the time the GAO requested cost data on the C–5A, Lockheed officials already knew the Air Force estimates and the Air Force knew they knew. Their release could be compromising only in that it would publicize the extent of the overrun on the C–5A program and embarrass those responsible for it.

During further hearings of the Proxmire subcommittee in January, 1969, Representative Martha Griffiths of Michigan became upset at the Air Force's refusal to supply the GAO with the C–5A cost estimates in order to "protect" Lockheed. She insisted that since Lockheed was no longer bidding against another company, there was no reason to keep the cost figures secret. "They have a contract," she told the director of the GAO's Defense Division. "You have a complete right to the information, and I would demand to exercise the right, and I think Congress has the right to know that . . . The person to protect is the American taxpayer. We deserve to be protected, not Lockheed." [4]

After considerable badgering by the GAO, the Air Force finally agreed to release the cost data on the condition that it not be made public — a meaningless offer, since the Air Force knew that Senator Proxmire had asked the GAO to obtain the information for use in public hearings of his Subcommittee on Economy in Government. The GAO refused to accept the offer on these grounds. Meanwhile, GAO field investigators had been trying in vain to obtain cost data directly from Lockheed, but Lockheed officials also refused, telling them to write to the C–5 System Program Office at the Air Force Systems Command in Dayton, Ohio. GAO requested the data from the SPO, but received no reply at all.

Finally, after direct written requests from Senator Proxmire to

Clark Clifford (who had replaced McNamara as Secretary of Defense) and from GAO Comptroller General Elmer Staats to Air Force Secretary Harold Brown, the Air Force finally gave in. After two months of futile correspondence, and more significantly, two days before the Proxmire hearing, Assistant Secretary Robert Charles sent the GAO a brief and incomplete cost summary of the C-5A program, explaining that "circumstances of the negotiations now make it possible to release the data." As he must have known, the GAO had no time to analyze even this sketchy summary in the two days before the hearing. (When the GAO finally submitted its full report on the C-5A to Proxmire's committee several months later, it read more like a Lockheed annual report than a critical investigation. It relied almost completely on cost figures supplied by either the Air Force or Lockheed. Proxmire found in it "very little evidence that the GAO conducted its own audits or made its own analysis.")

During the weeks that Air Force officials were busy putting off the GAO, they were also hurrying to reach a decision on the option to buy the 57 planes in Run B. According to the contract they had until the end of January, 1969, to exercise this option and could have easily arranged for an extension from Lockheed. While there were excellent reasons for delaying this decision — the main one being that at this point the Air Force had almost no idea what the planes would cost — there were also some pressing strategic reasons to act, and quickly. These had more to do with bureaucratic and corporate strategy than with defense strategy.

First of all the Air Force generals wanted the planes. Second, Lockheed, its subcontractors, and the 125,000 men who worked for them expected to build more planes. As *Business Week* had reported on the option back in 1965, "the Air Force is almost certain to exercise this, and eventually is expected to order even more." [5] (The contract had another option, to be exercised in 1970, for a third production run of 85 more planes.) Lockheed not only expected the follow-on order for Run B — the company had to have it. With costs already far above those set in the contract target, without the compensation of the repricing formula to boost the prices on Run B, the company would wind up roughly $670 million in debt by the end of Run A if the Air Force decided against Run B. This could send the company into bankruptcy. Faced with that prospect, Lockheed would probably have to terminate the contract, leaving the Air Force with what one USAF official described as "great big piles of aircraft in varying stages of completion, and I am not quite sure what you would do with them."

Back in Washington, there were even more compelling grounds for a hasty decision on Run B — the prospect of embarrassing revelations by the GAO and Fitzgerald at Proxmire's imminent hearings. These might have led Congress to try to stop the follow-on order. (Proxmire had already asked Defense Secretary Clifford to delay the decision until the GAO completed its investigation and reported to Congress.) In addition to the threat from Congress, the Air Force faced another threat from the White House, which would have a new resident on January 20. One of the new resident's customary prerogatives is holding up pending decisions on major programs until he has had a chance to examine them. For this reason the closing days of outgoing administrations are generally filled with feverish activity, trying to pass out as many jobs, award as many contracts, fulfill as many promises, and do as many favors as possible.

The Air Force must have realized that if it waited until the end of January before exercising its option on Run B, the publicity from the Proxmire hearings might prompt the new President to delay or even decide against the purchase of more planes.

Thus, on the morning of January 16, 1969, four days before Richard Nixon took office, and only hours before the GAO, Ernest Fitzgerald, and Robert Charles testified before the January session of the Proxmire subcommittee, the Air Force quietly placed its order for Run B. When a staff aide informed Proxmire of this move, just as he began to question the GAO's Assistant Comptroller General, he was shocked. He was not the only one struck by the timing of the decision: *Armed Forces Journal,* a normally pro-military publication, reported: "With what amounted to embarrassing haste, DoD last week exercised one of its options for more C–5A's — after giving Congress and the GAO only the barest of details on its long-promised findings about the C–5A cost overruns." [6]

Had Proxmire and other critics been able to read the fine print in the supplemental contract for Run B, they would have found something even more upsetting than the haste with which the Air Force exercised its option. A year and a half later, some law students doing research on military contracts noticed that the supplemental contract contained a revision of the original contract, extending the repricing formula to Run A, as well as Run B. At the time this revision was inserted (reportedly by Robert Charles) in the supposedly "fixed price" C–5A contract, the Air Force Office of Financial Management estimated it would add nearly $300 million to the cost of the C–5A program. When the revision was finally revealed, in August, 1970, the Air Force at first claimed it had been discussed in a USAF report on the C–5A issued in July, 1969, but somehow that section had then been dropped from the report. Both Lockheed and Air Force denied that the revision increased the payments for the C–5A. The Air Force claimed the provision only "changed the timing of repricing" by spreading the repricing payments over the total production run instead of waiting until Run B. A Lockheed spokesman explained the revision as merely designed to clear up an "ambiguity" in the original contract.[7]

In announcing its order for Run B, the Air Force obviously expected some criticism. Conceding that the plane's cost had risen well above original estimates, Secretary Clifford said he had concluded that the purchase of the additional planes would nevertheless be "in the national interest." [8] (Careful readers will recall this as the second major decision on the C–5A to be justified on the grounds of "national interest." The first was the decision to overrule the Source Selection Board and give the contract to Lockheed.) Although the phrase could probably be translated as "keeping Lockheed alive," its effectiveness lies in its very vagueness, for it offers critics nothing specific enough to attack. Besides, who can attack anything that is "in the national interest"?

The new Air Force arrangement with Lockheed (according to the Air Force) consisted of an order for the first 23 planes in Run B, with the understanding that, pending authorization of funds by Congress, it would decide upon the remaining 34 planes later in the year. The virtue of this arrangement was that it gave the impression of caution and thrift, which the Air Force obviously hoped would offset the criticism expected when the cost overrun for Run A became known. That impression of thrift, however, did not impress everyone. At a congressional hearing a few months later, Senator Howard Cannon (Dem.-Nev.) told an Air Force general that it was "common knowledge" that "you intended to buy at least 120 if Congress approves, so I do not think that this cutoff [at 81 planes] was fooling anyone, even yourselves." [9]

The question of who was fooling whom is hardly as rhetorical as it seems, for there was considerable difference of opinion between the Air Force, Lockheed, and Congress over just what the option meant in terms of the government's obligation to Lockheed. According to Robert Moot, the new Comptroller for the Defense Department, the order for more planes depended specifically on the authorization of funds by Congress. In June, 1969, General Duward Crow, by then Comptroller of the Air Force, told the Senate Armed Services Committee, "We have not contracted for those 23." Except for a piddling $50 million worth of "long-lead items" (components which required lengthy advance notice to insure their availability), said General Crow, the Air Force had only committed itself to "the right to buy" the planes.[10] That same afternoon, however, before the same committee, Lockheed's chairman of the board, Daniel Haughton, insisted that the Air Force had in fact exercised this right to buy when it exercised the option, pending congressional authorization. Pennsylvania's freshman senator Richard Schweiker, one of the few congressmen who had actually bothered to examine the C–5A contract, agreed, and felt that the option was even more binding. "As I read the contract," Schweiker told Haughton, "it says that the supplemental option [for Run B] is binding pending receipt of a letter from Secretary Brown." [11] Since Secretary Brown had indeed sent Lockheed a letter of confirmation on January 18, and since the contract did not mention congressional authorization, the Air Force may have in fact legally ordered the additional planes. Contrary to the testimony of General Crow, it had done so without authorization from Congress and without any congressional appropriation to pay for them.

Anyone surprised at such independent action by the Defense Department should not be, for it happens all the time, whether or not most congressmen realize it. The only surprising aspect of this unauthorized order for more C–5As is the fact that Congress found out about it. Normally there would be no special hearings on a major program. It would simply be buried along with hundreds of other million or billion dollar items in the annual military appropriation bill.

In addition to being hasty, disingenuous, and furtive, the Air Force decision to buy more C–5As can be criticized on other significant grounds. Most important is the question of whether there was any need for them. The planes in Run A would be enough for three squadrons, and the Air Force had been counting on the 57 planes of Run B to provide a total of six squadrons. Although USAF generals insisted upon their need for all six, and were already busy planning their deployment, other officials at the Pentagon had some doubts about the necessity of even a fourth squadron.

In a paper prepared in the fall of 1968, several months before the option came up, the Office of Systems Analysis concluded that a fourth squadron of C–5As was not worth the money required to buy them. Noting that cost estimates had risen far above the original contract price, the paper stated that the Air Force could get the same airlift capacity for much less money by making more intensive use of the three squadrons already ordered in Run A. Pointing out that the Air Force planned to use the C–5As only a few hours each day, the OSA suggested calling up extra flight crews from the National Guard or reserves, which would enable each plane to be utilized more fully. Over a ten-year period, the expense of these extra crews would amount to only one-seventh the cost of building and operating a fourth squadron of C–5As.[12]

Like most other official documents that questioned the cost or necessity of the C–5A, this Systems Analysis report was immediately classified. Its existence only emerged nearly a year later when an enterprising reporter, Bernard Nossiter of the *Washington Post,* got wind of it. Apparently Air Force Secretary Brown heard about it too, for in a memo dated October 15, 1968, he wrote: "the Air Force does not have to have Run B. Other alternatives could be pursued." [13]

In addition to more intensive utilization of the first three squadrons of Run A, there was another reasonable alternative that might have been pursued, but wasn't — Boeing's 747. Using basically the same design submitted in its bid for the C-5A contract, Boeing had gone ahead since that time and with private financing developed what is now its successful new passenger liner, the 747. Facing many of the same problems that drove Lockheed's cost up on the C-5A, Boeing somehow managed to produce its commercial version for very close to its original bid price on the C-5A. The reasons for this may include more efficient management and production, but one of them must certainly be the fact that the airlines which had taken options on the 747 would have simply refused to buy them if they had wound up costing more than twice the original price. Commercial customers, unlike the Air Force, must spend their own money and are therefore not as understanding as the Defense Department when confronted by huge cost overruns. As a result, cost overruns somehow do not occur in commercial aerospace contracts anywhere near as often as they do on defense contracts. And when they do occur, they are rarely so large. Ernest Fitzgerald, who as an industrial efficiency expert has studied civilian and defense industry for many years, estimates that defense contractors generally have about 50 per cent more "fat" in their operations than similar firms doing civilian work.

As the time for the C-5A option approached, no one at the Air Force ever bothered to check with Boeing on the possibility of buying 747s instead of additional C-5As, despite the fact that at $22 million apiece they represented a great bargain compared to Lockheed's C-5A, then estimated at roughly $45 million each. Finally Boeing officials came to see Secretary Brown at the Pentagon with a proposal for a cargo version called the 747B. Not only would it cost less than half as much as the C–5A, but it had a faster cruising speed and could carry a heavier payload. The Air Force argued that the 747B did not have the C–5A's air-drop, short-landing, and roll-on loading capabilities, and that it could not handle out-size items of military cargo for which the C–5A had been designed. (Since then Boeing has designed into its 747B a self-loading device superior in many respects to the C–5A's built-in ramps, plus the capability to operate into a 4000-foot unpaved runway.) Boeing executives admitted the 747B lacked some of the C–5A's specialized features, but questioned whether the Defense Department needed these expensive extras on its entire air cargo fleet. They pointed out that 90 per cent of all military air freight today is "containerized or palletized" cargo, which would fit as easily into the 747B as the C–5A. None of their arguments had much effect.[14]

Anyone interested in a more dramatic insight into the Air Force decision-making process would have enjoyed the following exchange which took place several months later when Robert Charles was questioned about the C–5A option by Representative Robert Leggett of California:

> Mr. Leggett: Prior to the time you exercised your option to buy what you consider to be 23 aircraft under Run B, did you run a cost estimate comparison with the 747?
> Mr. Charles: Did I — no, sir.
> Mr. Leggett: I see. Did the Air Force run a cost-effectiveness comparison with the 747?
> Mr. Charles: I imagine so.

Mr. Leggett reminded Mr. Charles that he had been defending the cost growth on the C–5A partly on the grounds that as a result of design changes it had become a bigger plane than specified in the original contract. The congressman then pointed out that although the 747 was much cheaper than the C–5A, it was also heavier.

> Mr. Charles: I'm not certain that it is heavier. I did not think it was heavier.
>
> Mr. Leggett: As I recall the figures it was on the order of 785,000 pounds as compared to a little over 700,000 pounds for the C–5A.
>
> Mr. Charles: You may be right. I have not heard that. I don't think it is right.
>
> Mr. Leggett: Then if you haven't heard it, you have not rationalized how they can produce more pounds of that airplane for that price than Lockheed can.
>
> Mr. Charles: I have no idea what Boeing's pricing policy is.

Mr. Leggett then asked Mr. Charles how he could have recommended exercising the option for more C–5As without thoroughly reviewing the cost and performance capabilities of the 747. Charles replied that the 747 could not do several things the C–5A could do, particularly in the way of handling heavy equipment.

> Mr. Leggett: Are you acquainted with the estimates to convert the 747 to carry heavy equipment and heavy cargo?
>
> Mr. Charles: I am not.
>
> Mr. Leggett: Did you make an investigation?
>
> Mr. Charles: No, I did not.
>
> Mr. Leggett: Did you think it reasonable you should make an investigation?
>
> Mr. Charles: No, I did not. It was not my responsibility.[15]

Even allowing for this kind of buck-passing, which goes on in any bureaucracy, the cost of the C–5As was certainly part of Mr. Charles' responsibility. Yet at the time the Air Force exercised its option for more of them he seems to have been remarkably hazy about their eventual price, despite numerous Air Force cost studies on the subject. When pressed by Senator Proxmire for the cost per plane of the 23 planes in the new order, Charles gave an estimate of $23.5 million each, which would not have been too far from the unit price in the original contract. However, in the official Air Force estimates he supplied shortly afterward for Proxmire's subcommittee record, the unit price was $33.5 million, excluding spare parts and other "extras." When Charles was unable to offer an estimate at the hearing for the total cost of the C–5A program including spare parts, ground support, and other "extras" that were part of the contract, Proxmire was amazed. (These extras ultimately came to nearly $1 billion.) "I cannot understand why you cannot give us this," he told Charles. "You know more about this program than any other living man, according to everybody I have talked to. It is your program. It is your total operation, and I cannot understand how you cannot give us that figure."

The real reason that Charles could not answer was that despite its "official" estimates (which proved to be grossly underestimated) the Air Force actually had almost no idea what the C–5As would cost when it exercised the option. Some of the ignorance and confusion on the price of the plane can be attributed to the fact that at this time Lockheed had completed assembly on only four of the giant transports, with 17 others in what a company official described as "bits and pieces." Instead of being an excuse for ignorance and confusion, however, this fact should have been sufficient reason to delay the option until further along in the program when the costs could be more accurately estimated.

CHAPTER FIVE

Committees

"We can proceed with the assurance that costs are reasonable, and the taxpayer will be getting a good return for his investment."

Robert Seamans,
Secretary of the Air Force

EVER SINCE COMMITTEES became a standard part of civic, corporate, and social machinery in this country, there has been a popular belief that nothing ever gets done by them. However true this may be for the rest of man's affairs, it does not apply to Congress. Most work of any significance there is done by committees before the bills come before the full House or Senate for a vote.

The jurisdiction and effectiveness of a congressional committee, like that of any committee, depend to a great extent on the ability and will of its members, particularly its chairman. As a result, the responsibilities of the various committees on Capitol Hill often overlap and conflict. Just as you can't determine the quality of a book by its cover, you can't always predict the concerns of a congressional committee by its title. One would expect, for example, that the House and Senate Armed Services Committees would cover all legislation dealing with military affairs, and as far as the Defense Department is concerned, they do. But while these two committees prepare the annual military procurement bills, they rarely initiate any critical investigation of military spending. The reason for this is a matter of inclination rather than jurisdiction. The chairmen of the two Armed Services Committees have traditionally been the military's staunchest friends and protectors on Capitol Hill. In turn, the military services have traditionally rewarded these chairmen, as well as ranking committee members, with such marks of affection as military installations and defense contracts for their home states or districts.

The Armed Services Committee chairmen and their staffs prepare most legislation by dealing directly with the service secretaries, chiefs of staff, and other top DoD officials, often without consulting individual committee members. Since the committee's information-gathering is done by staff aides who are completely controlled by the chairman, individual members normally have access only to such information as the chairman permits. Even if they come up with something on their own that might embarrass the Pentagon, they may not get a chance to use it, because the chairman can usually squelch any private investigations and can always cut members off during committee hearings.

Those who hope for critical analysis of defense spending must look elsewhere than to the House or Senate Armed Services Committees. Fortunately, two other congressional subcommittees have sufficient jurisdiction and interest to examine defense spending from time to time — the Joint Economic Committee's Subcommittee on Economy in Government and the House Government Operations Committee's Subcommittee on Military Operations. These two groups have certain problems, however, which make their scrutiny of the Defense budget difficult. Their own budgets and staff are minuscule compared to those of the Armed Services Committees. The Military Operations Subcommittee has a staff of five, and the Subcommittee on Economy in Government has only one aide who devotes most of his time to military affairs. The greatest problem for these subcommittees in gathering information is not a matter of understaffing, however. Because they have had the temerity to criticize the Defense establishment, the Pentagon has become increasingly uncooperative in responding to their requests for information. This makes their work not only difficult, but often impossible.

As Chairman of the Subcommittee on Economy in Government, Senator William Proxmire controls his hearings just as carefully as the chairmen of the Armed Services Committees do theirs, but the results are strikingly different. A graduate of Yale, Harvard Business School, and Harvard's Graduate School of Public Administration, the senior senator from Wisconsin has become one of the Senate's most outspoken liberals, and a frequent critic of defense spending. After several years in the state legislature, and three unsuccessful tries for the governorship, he won a special election in 1957 to fill the unexpired term of the late Senator Joe McCarthy. With the defeat of his mentor, Senator Paul Douglas (Dem-Ill.), in 1966, Proxmire took over Douglas' chairmanship of the subcommittee, a position which has brought him sufficient prominence to be frequently mentioned as a "dark horse" candidate for the presidency. A former collegiate boxing champion, Proxmire, now 55, stays in shape by running nearly five miles each day from his home to Capitol Hill. He displays the same energy during his subcommittee hearings.

While Proxmire has received most of the publicity for the subcommittee's investigations, the man most responsible for them is Richard Kaufman, the subcommittee's young lawyer-economist, who almost single-handedly organizes its hearings on military spending. For several months in 1968, Kaufman had been preparing for a series of hearings on military procurement. During interviews with dozens of prospective witnesses, both in and outside the Pentagon, many people wished him well, but refused to testify in public. There was, says Kaufman, "a definite environment of fear and intimidation." One of the few Pentagon officials who agreed to testify was Ernest Fitzgerald, and even he had to request approval from his superiors before agreeing to do so.

Early in the fall of 1968, by then aware that the Proxmire subcommittee was planning hearings on defense spending, the Pentagon invited Kaufman to a special briefing on procurement. High-ranking representatives from the three services described for him their major weapon programs. Several officials referred specifically to the C–5A contract as a model of defense procurement, but refused to disclose current estimates on the program's cost. Curious, Kaufman did some sniffing, and heard rumors about a huge cost overrun on the C–5A. He had heard about Fitzgerald and asked him if he would testify before the subcommittee. Fitzgerald agreed, and did, in November, 1968.

Had Fitzgerald not testified when he did, the C–5A cost overrun might have remained hidden for some time, considering the testimony of other Pentagon officials. For example, the day before, when Proxmire asked John Malloy, Deputy Assistant Secretary of Defense for Procurement, several questions about the C–5A contract — one of the biggest items within Malloy's jurisdiction — Malloy was unable to supply any information. He claimed he was "not intimately familiar with that contract." [1]

The next committee to look into the C–5A affair was the House Subcommittee on Military Operations. Despite its clear jurisdiction in such matters, this subcommittee has one serious impediment — its chairman, Representative Chet Holifield (Dem.-Cal.). Unlike Proxmire, Holifield has never shown much interest in cutting defense costs. For example, when Defense Secretary Melvin Laird began suggesting his department's budget could be gradually cut to $60 billion over a five-year period, Holifield immediately declared that the military budget "can not safely fall much below the $70 billion level." [2] Some years ago, when the General Accounting Office began probing into profits in the missile industry, the industry's Washington lobbyists protested to Holifield. He responded by calling for an investigation not of missile profits, but of the GAO itself.[3] In addition to his generally hawkish nature, Holifield's opposition to cutting defense spending may be motivated by the fact that several of the country's biggest missile contractors, North American, Aerojet-General, and Textron — are located in his Southern California district.

By the time Holifield's subcommittee took up the C–5A affair, in April, 1969, it had become such a hot potato that no one from the Pentagon wanted to claim responsibility for it. The subcommittee's administrative chief, Herbert Roback, asked Aaron Racusin, Deputy Assistant Secretary of the Air Force for Procurement, if his office had been responsible for the direction of the C–5A program. In a display of linguistic ingenuity, Racusin replied, "We have retained visibility of technical changes, technical development, and cost development. I would not be prepared to say that we are directing action." Roback could only mutter, "There seems to be a credibility gap in visibility on the C–5." [4]

Roback then questioned Colonel Kenneth Beckman, head of the Air Force's C–5 System Program Office, on the matter of concealment of the cost overrun. Roback wanted to know why the Air Force had told Congress a year before that there was no cost overrun on the C–5A, when there had already been official reports that the program was running far above the original cost estimates. Colonel Beckman recalled that at that time "we had feelings that it might, but we could not justify those feelings."

> Mr. Roback: Was it your understanding that the contractor was reluctant to make the prices visible at that time, because this might complicate your buying plans?
> Col. Beckman: I would have to say that we had that feeling, sir.
> Mr. Roback: Let me ask you this question: When you did identify, around the middle of the year, that there was going to be a substantial cost overrun, why did you not report that information?

Colonel Beckman insisted the overrun figures had been reported "to the highest levels," but only "verbally." Later they appeared in quarterly "Selected Acquisition Reports" that received extremely limited but "appropriate distribution within the Department of Defense." As Colonel Beckman summed up, "the various people . . . who were close to the program, and had a need to know, were fully informed." [5] To anyone following his testimony, it was clear that poor Colonel Beckman was trying to cover up for the fact that the Air Force had covered up the C–5A cost overrun.

The only one of the subcommittee's seven members who seemed genuinely interested in probing the C–5A affair was Representative William Moorhead (Dem.-Pa.), who had learned about the plane through his membership on the Proxmire subcommittee. Unlike Proxmire, Moorhead was hardly a household name before his contact with the C–5A. A graduate of Yale and Harvard Law School, he had given up a prosperous Pittsburgh law practice to run for Congress in 1959. For ten years, in the words of one Washington reporter, Moorhead had served his district "with dignity and obscurity, giving parties of note at his Georgetown home, and sponsoring measures no more controversial than a foundation for arts and humanities."

Moorhead might have remained in relative obscurity and ruffled no feathers at the Pentagon had it not been for his 32-year-old legislative aide, Peter Stockton. A former economist with the Bureau of the Budget, Stockton had been intrigued during the Proxmire hearings by how the C–5A cost overrun had disappeared from the Air Force reports. On behalf of Congressman Moorhead he pressed the GAO to find out, and also did some research on his own. The GAO had trouble getting anything out of the Air Force, but finally a reluctant phone call from Comptroller General Elmer Staats to Air Force Secretary Robert Seamans, who had replaced Harold Brown, forced the Air Force to admit that Assistant Secretary Charles had ordered the C–5 System Program Office to delete the cost overrun information from its reports.[6]

Armed with this and other documents obtained from the GAO, ex-lawyer Moorhead put the Air Force witnesses at the otherwise friendly Military Operations hearings through a rugged cross-examination full of "Are you familiar with . . ." and "Is it not true that . . . ?" Under his questioning, the embarrassed Air Force officials gave further evidence of concealment of the cost overrun. Chairman Holifield, visibly upset at the way the hearings were getting out of his control, tried to suggest that the information unearthed by Moorhead was classified, and implied its disclosure might damage national security. When the Air Force witnesses themselves denied the documents were classified, Holifield tried to browbeat Moorhead on how he had obtained them, as though Moorhead himself was under investigation instead of the Air Force and the C–5A. Holifield made it quite clear that Moorhead's disclosures were his own doing, and not the work of the subcommittee.

While the hearings of the Proxmire and Military Operations subcommittees produced considerable publicity on the C–5A scandal, neither was able to achieve any concrete results, since both are "study" rather than "legislative" bodies. Unlike the House and Senate Armed Services Committees, which actually draft and control bills on military matters, these two subcommittees can merely report to Congress and recommend legislation. Thus, if Congress were to actually do anything about the C–5A affair, it would normally have to be done by either of the Armed Services Committees. To anyone familiar with these committees, such action was not likely.

Six months passed after Fitzgerald's first disclosure of the $2 billion C–5A overrun before either Armed Services Committee bothered to look into the matter, and then only because they happened to be holding their annual hearings on military procurement. In fact, had it not been for the extraordinary amount of public controversy surrounding the plane, they probably would have treated it as they generally treated such cost overruns in the past — by ignoring them and simply voting whatever funds the services requested.

On June 3 and 4, 1969, the Senate Armed Services Committee (SASC) held special hearings on the C–5A. Like political trials in Russia, the purpose of such investigations generally has nothing to do with determining innocence or guilt, or even fixing responsibility. They are basically public rituals designed to present an image of objectivity. They create the appearance of congressional concern about something that has embarrassed Congress. Committee members often have little knowledge about the particular subject under examination, and little desire to actually do much about it. The hearings give the Pentagon an opportunity to present its version of the story in a friendly atmosphere, usually without fear of unpleasant cross-examination.

To insure such an atmosphere for its C–5A hearings, the SASC invited only Air Force and Lockheed officials. Lockheed's board chairman, Daniel Haughton, who had refused to appear before the more critical Proxmire subcommittee, readily accepted the SASC invitation. The committee pointedly did not invite the only man likely to present any unpleasant testimony — Ernest Fitzgerald. Such exclusion of dissent is standard practice at SASC hearings. When the committee held secret hearings in 1968 on the question of whether to deploy the ABM, only pro-ABM witnesses appeared. The committee refused to hear testimony from two dozen anti-ABM scientists, including four former presidential advisers.

The main reason Pentagon and industry witnesses generally feel confident of an amiable atmosphere at SASC hearings is because they have confidence in its chairman, Senator John Stennis (Dem.-Miss.). Their confidence is well placed. The courtly senator from Kemper County, Mississippi, has long been a faithful ally of the military and has rarely been critical of defense spending. Now 69, Stennis waited many years as the SASC's second-ranking Democrat behind former chairman Richard Russell. In 1969, the 71-year-old Russell finally relinquished his 16-year rule of the SASC to become chairman of the Appropriations Committee, upon the retirement of 91-year-old Carl Hayden (Dem.-Ariz.). Though somewhat more tolerant of dissent than Russell, Stennis nonetheless usually gets his way on anything of importance in the committee and generally follows the advice of the military men at the Pentagon. When he moved up to the SASC's chairmanship, instead of giving up his leadership of its influential Subcommittee on Military Preparedness to Senator Stuart Symington (Dem.-Mo.), the next-ranking and more liberal Democratic member, he retained it himself.

The Pentagon and the defense industry lost no time in showing their respect for the new SASC chairman. In March, 1969, two weeks before the committee opened hearings on the fiscal 1970 military budget, nearly every top DoD official from Secretary Laird and the Joint Chiefs of Staff on down showed up for a testimonial dinner for Stennis in Jackson, Mississippi. Air Force jets ferried congressional dignitaries down from Washington, D.C., and dozens of defense industry executives arrived in their company planes. Mississippians in the gathering, wondering whether their native son's new power would bring military bases and defense contracts to their relatively barren state, heard encouraging words from House Armed Services Committee chairman L. Mendel Rivers. Clearly pleased to have a fellow

Southerner guiding military affairs in the Senate, Rivers proclaimed: "I don't believe the Yankees will pick a fight with us
again, because when we get through there'll be precious few
installations left North of the Mason-Dixon Line." [7]

Stennis probably felt a bit uncomfortable at this insinuation
that he would use his new position to bring contracts and bases
to Mississippi. In the opinion of a Washington reporter who has
studied the SASC chairman's career, Stennis "clearly lacks Mendel
Rivers's appetite for pork." [8] Whether he tries or not, however, it
may happen anyway. In 1968, just before Stennis became chairman, Litton Industries began work on a $130 million shipyard in
Pascagoula, Mississippi (financed by the state and leased to
Litton on generous terms), which now employs more than 5000
men. In the summer of 1970 Litton won the biggest Navy shipbuilding plum in years — a $2 billion contract to build a new
class (DD–963) of destroyers.

If the Air Force and Lockheed had to pick a jury to hear the
case of the C–5A, they could hardly have picked a generally
friendlier group than the Senate Armed Services Committee. The
ranking Democrat on the 18-member committee was Senator Russell, obviously unlikely to criticize a contract for which he had
been largely responsible. Perhaps to save himself embarrassment,
or because his health had been fragile, Mr. Russell did not
attend the SASC hearings on the C–5A. Six other members were
also unable or did not bother to attend: Senators Jackson of
Washington, Ervin of North Carolina, Inouye of Hawaii, Tower
of Texas, Dominick of Colorado, and Brooke of Massachusetts.
Of the remaining ten members who attended the hearings, only
two — Howard Cannon of Nevada and Richard Schweiker of
Pennsylvania — questioned the witnesses with any vigor, despite
numerous gaps, obvious contradictions, and considerable confusion in their testimony. The generally friendly hosts included

Senators Stuart Symington of Missouri, a former Secretary of the Air Force; Harry Byrd Jr. of Virginia; Margaret Chase Smith of Maine; Strom Thurmond of South Carolina, a major general in the Army Reserve; George Murphy of California; and Barry Goldwater of Arizona.

When he left the Senate in 1964 to run against Lyndon Johnson for the presidency, Goldwater gave up his position as a ranking GOP member of the SASC. But upon his reelection to the Senate in 1968, he was quickly reappointed to the committee because of his supposed expertise in military matters. Like Senator Cannon, he maintains active flight status as a major general in the Air Force Reserve. For this reason, immediately after the SASC hearings closed, chairman Stennis sent Goldwater down to Marietta, Georgia, to personally inspect the plane. Goldwater actually piloted one of the test C–5As and returned with a predictably glowing report. Major General Goldwater's objectivity in such matters did not impress Murray Kempton in an article on the C–5A in *The New York Review of Books*. Kempton wrote that if the Air Force told Goldwater to test-fly an elephant, "he would get on board and dismount, attesting that he had flown Beechcraft that were harder to handle." [9]

Air Force Secretary Robert Seamans opened the C–5A hearings June 3, 1969, with a 28-page statement giving the Pentagon's official version of the C–5A program. When he got around to the subject of cost, Seamans admitted the program might have an overrun "upward of a billion dollars, probably on the order of a billion and a half," [10] but he assured the committee the plane would be "worth its cost." Because of all the controversy over the plane, Seamans announced that Philip Whittaker, who had just replaced Robert Charles as Assistant Air Force Secretary in charge of procurement, was conducting a complete and "searching" review of the entire C–5A program.

Seamans and Whittaker managed to avoid most of the difficult questions put to them by committee members on the grounds that they had not been involved in the C–5A program at the time of the contract or the concealment of the overrun. Some committee members even expressed sympathy for their plight, in being burdened with such an expensive scandal not of their own making. Much of their testimony, however, gave the impression that even if they had been around at the time, things would not have turned out differently. For example, when Senator Byrd asked Secretary Seamans if he felt "those who make contracts on behalf of the taxpayers are obligated to strike a hard bargain with the contractors?" Seamans replied, "I concur that they must strike a fair bargain. I am not certain what you mean by a hard bargain . . . I don't believe that the word "hard" should imply catastrophic losses."

> Senator Byrd: I don't think the word should necessarily imply any losses. What I am speaking of when I say "hard," I mean that the taxpayers are fully and adequately protected.
> Secretary Seamans: I would certainly agree with that, Senator Byrd.
> Senator Byrd: Does the Lockheed contract which we have been discussing today fit into that category?
> Secretary Seamans: In my view it does . . .
> Senator Byrd: I am not certain.

Secretary Seamans stressed the importance of a "contractual arrangement where there is good communication back and forth, where there is flexibility in the arrangement to take into account changes that may occur either technically or in requirements." But Senator Byrd insisted, "the contracting parties can have a good rapport and fine working relationships, and still strike a hard contract, one to the other."

Most of the questioning followed this general level. Few of the committee members knew enough about the C–5A to ask specific questions, despite the fact that over the past few years they had already approved the spending of more than $2 billion on the program. Several members seemed unaware of how many planes had been ordered and had no idea of their cost. While some of this ignorance was probably due to the press of other legislative interests, much of it is normal for SASC hearings. The committee members are usually concerned about the need for and effective-ness of various weapons in the defense budget, but they have never been particularly concerned about price.

The few members who seemed genuinely upset about the cost overrun on the C–5A were unable to learn much about it from this hearing. The Air Force witnesses, though properly concerned, and just sufficiently contrite, did little but add to the confusion. They threw up a smokescreen of complicated charts, graphs, figures, and explanations that left the committee openly be-wildered. They answered most specific or potentially embar-rassing questions with such standard ploys as "that point is now under review" or "we will supply that later for the record." Somehow, the most important information could not be deter-mined just then: a report was not yet completed; construction had not yet reached that stage; new cost estimates would not be ready until the following month.

Despite this lack of cooperation from the Air Force, a few committee members had seen enough about the C–5A in the newspapers to be concerned at what they felt was an attempt to cover up the cost overrun. They expressed amazement that a program which the Air Force had described to Congress only a year before as "within the range of the contract target" could suddenly be $1 to $2 billion over that target. Whenever they confronted the Air Force witnesses with this "sudden" cost growth, however, they were told, "Well, first we have to put this thing in perspective," or were given some other evasive generali-

ties. The Air Force perspective usually meant more confusion.
When Senator Howard Cannon asked Assistant Secretary Whittaker if the Air Force had had "timely notice that there were going to be cost overruns on this contract," Whittaker simply replied, "Yes, sir." Cannon, a former Las Vegas city attorney, did not find this very helpful. "Is that the end of your answer?" he asked. Whittaker tried to explain that although there had been several cost reviews that showed "indications" of an overrun, they had not been "conclusive." Cannon was appalled. "You say you had indications in 1966 and in 1967 that you were going to have these cost overruns [but] apparently all you did is question the estimates and make more studies."

Even Senator George Murphy, a normally uncritical supporter of the military, could not swallow the Air Force story on the overrun. "It seems to me shocking," he told General Crow, the Air Force Comptroller, "that in this day of computers we have to wait so long to find out that we have been so far under [sic] budget . . . You know, at one point, General, I was vice-president of a large studio where we had eighteen companies shooting television shows at one time, and we had to know every afternoon exactly at three o'clock where we stood. And if we did not know, we could have been out of business by the next morning. I think the Defense Department has a parallel case, and I think that they ought to have another look at the way they keep track of things."

Except for a few remarks like these, most of the hearings passed easily enough for the Air Force witnesses, and they probably congratulated themselves for having made an effective case. Summarizing their official position for chairman Stennis, Secretary Seamans even expressed pride in the Air Force's handling of the C–5A program: "In spite of these difficulties, I have no question but that within this contract, with suitable negotiations, we can work with Lockheed. We can provide an entirely satisfactory aircraft that will do the job that was originally laid out. And we can proceed with the assurance that costs are reasonable, and the taxpayer will be getting a good return for his investment."

Stennis apparently agreed with this opinion. While he did suggest that someone ought to "look further now into this contract," he claimed to be "mighty well impressed with the Air Force's capability in this matter." He was also mighty well impressed with Lockheed's chairman Daniel Haughton and Lockheed-Georgia's president Thomas May, whose testimony he found "very clear." How anyone could have been impressed with the clarity of statements by both the Air Force and Lockheed is surprising, since they contradicted each other on nearly every major aspect of the C–5A contract.

Mr. Haughton claimed the Air Force had exercised its option for the 57 planes of Run B, and that his company had a firm contract for them. Air Force witnesses claimed they had not yet ordered the planes. The Air Force estimated the cost of the total program at $4.6 billion, but Lockheed put the figure somewhere "over five billion." The Air Force insisted that no money had yet been spent on Run B, but Mr. May informed the committee that Lockheed-Georgia had already received nearly $50 million for long-lead time items for Run B. The Air Force claimed that $500 million of the C–5A cost overrun was due to inflation. Lockheed officials attributed $627 million to inflation. The Air Force told the SASC that Lockheed would lose $285 million on the entire program. Lockheed claimed it would lose only $13 million and might even manage to "break even, or come out slightly ahead."

To try and clear up some of the confusion, the committee recalled the Air Force witnesses, and freshman Senator Richard Schweiker asked them to explain some of the most glaring conflicts that had emerged in the testimony. The Air Force attempts to clarify matters only increased the confusion. After one particularly incomprehensible explanation, General Crow concluded, "I don't think even the most severe critics of this method of contracting would really criticize it if they understood it fully." Senator Schweiker, who had made a futile attempt to follow General Crow's explanation, had the honesty to admit he was "one of those who do not understand fully . . . It seems to me you are really saying that none of these contracts amounts to a hill of beans, that basically we can tear them up at will."

CHAPTER SIX

Rivers Delivers

"I don't care what the contract says."

L. Mendel Rivers,
Chairman of the
House Armed Services Committee

PROBABLY EVERYONE except some of its members would agree that the Senate Armed Services Committee produced little more than confusion with its two-day investigation into the C–5A scandal. Some critics accused the committee of trying to whitewash the whole affair, while others felt the confusion was due to excessive haste. Those who felt that a longer inquiry might have produced more meaningful results would be wrong, however. The House Armed Services Committee (HASC) proved this by devoting more than five days to the C–5A affair, without learning much more than its counterpart in the Senate.

The man most responsible for the HASC's failure to conduct a real investigation of the C–5A was its chairman, the late L. Mendel Rivers of Charleston, South Carolina. His control over the committee staff was absolute. As one HASC member put it, "Mendel Rivers is the chairman, and he picks most of the Committee staff, and they think like Mendel."

The HASC staff and its hearings are both tightly run by chief counsel John Blandford, a brigadier general in the Marine Reserve, who shares chairman Rivers' views on military affairs. "My responsibility is not to the public," Blandford once told a reporter. "It is to the chairman alone." [1]

While slightly less slavish about it, most HASC members remained relatively loyal to chairman Rivers if they valued their own careers. Except for occasional floor speeches, which generally receive little coverage in the press, the only way most congressmen can capture public attention without paying for it is by conspicuous service on some subcommittee. Around election time, the chairmanship of even a minor subcommittee can be more valuable than the biggest campaign contribution. The chairman of the full committee has the sole power to make subcommittee assignments and also decides when and what the subcommittees will investigate. The hope of receiving choice subcommittee assignments keeps most congressmen loyal to their chairman.

No other chairman on Capitol Hill demanded greater loyalty from his committee members than Rivers. No more than five of the 40 members ever voted against him in committee meetings. These men earned themselves the title, "the Fearless Five," as well as the chairman's enmity. His anger could not be taken lightly. When one of the dissidents, Representative Otis Pike (Dem.-N.Y.), was in line to take over the chairmanship of the HASC's vital Special Investigations Subcommittee in 1969, Rivers quickly made himself chairman of the subcommittee and kicked Pike off it entirely. His vigilance over military affairs extended well beyond the HASC. When Representative William Moorhead remarked on the House floor that "some Members of Congress have dealt so long with the military and with the defense contractors that they begin to think they are without faults," Rivers summoned Moorhead to explain himself before the HASC. When Moorhead said he would be happy to do so in open session, Rivers dropped the matter.[2]

Because of the billions of dollars in annual military expenditures, no committee offers its chairman more power than the HASC, and no chairman wielded his power with more gusto than

Lucius Mendel Rivers. Although the HASC has 39 other members, nothing got into the annual military procurement bill without his approval. Billion-dollar projects could literally pass or fail on his whim.

While there was never any evidence that Rivers' approval could be bought with money, the services and several of the largest defense companies paid him handsomely in the currency most valuable to any politician — jobs and prestige. After Rivers took over the HASC chairmanship in 1965 from 81-year-old Carl Vinson of Georgia, several big defense firms (including General Electric and AVCO, both of which have major contracts on the C–5A) built plants in or near Charleston. Soon after it won the C–5A contract, Lockheed announced that it too would build a sub-assembly plant in Charleston. Rivers did not find any of this embarrassing.

The Pentagon has shown equal appreciation of Charleston's strategic location. Rivers' district now has an Air Force base, an Army supply depot, a Marine air station and recruit depot, a naval base, a naval air station, two naval hospitals, a Navy shipyard, and two submarine bases. Local wags say that if Charleston gets just one more military base it will sink. Nevertheless, when the Air Force had to pick a site for the first C–5A squadron, the choice soon narrowed down to Charleston Air Force Base.

The federal payroll in Rivers' district now runs well over $3 billion a year, and his influence hardly ends at the borders of his own district. "Without bragging," he once bragged, "I can say that I have sponsored ninety per cent of the military installations in this state." The Rivers campaign motto for many years used to be "Rivers Delivers," and for those Charleston voters who didn't get the message, there were reminders all over town. Route 52, known locally as Rivers Avenue, runs through Charleston to Rivers Gate, the entrance to Charleston AFB. A new housing project at the naval base is called Men-Riv Park. A few years ago grateful Charleston businessmen raised a fund to finance the erection of a bust of the chairman that now overlooks Rivers Avenue. When contributions ran short for the project, one company put up the rest of the money — Lockheed. The secretaries of the Army, Navy, and Air Force, along with dozens of other military and congressional dignitaries, showed up for the dedication of this statue, as they regularly did for any occasion held in the chairman's honor. On weekends the Air Force stood ready with private flights for Rivers between the Capitol and Charleston. It also provided overseas transportation for Rivers, friendly HASC members, and staff aides, who often find the need to inspect U.S. military installations in Paris, London, and Rome.[3]

To a Gumville, South Carolina, boy who never attained the rank of private (neither Rivers nor Stennis ever served in uniform), such marks of respect from the Pentagon meant a great deal. To the Pentagon they represented a profitable investment. Rivers remained a steadfast supporter of the military throughout his 29 years in Congress, and since he rose to the chairmanship of the HASC, relations between the committee and the Pentagon have been most cordial. "As far as he's concerned," said one HASC member of Rivers, "the military can do no wrong."

Because of such faith in the Pentagon's wisdom, Rivers had simply approved funds for the C–5A year after year until 1969, without even requesting a briefing on the program from the Air Force. Normally HASC members are expected to remain in a similar state of benign ignorance, but the C–5A cost overrun had become such a public scandal that several members began insisting the committee look into it. Rivers refused to allow a full-scale investigation, but reluctantly agreed to hold hearings on the matter. He vehemently denied press reports that he had been "forced" to do so by the threat of a mini-rebellion within the committee.

When Secretary of Defense Melvin Laird appeared before the

HASC in May, 1969, Rivers made it quite clear that he would not give anyone a hard time on the C–5A. "Those fellows over in the other body [the Senate] are going to beat this thing to death," he told Laird. "From where I sit, at least, you are getting a plane that is going to work, that is fulfilling a very urgent need." Secretary Laird, obviously pleased at this warm reception, replied simply, "We need the C–5A." [4]

When the matter of the cost overrun came up, Laird gave an estimate of $382 to $500 million. Rivers reminded him that the "people over in the other body are talking about two billion."

"They have not got the right information, Mr. Chairman," said Air Force Chief of Staff General John McConnell.

"We have an overrun problem here," Laird conceded, "but some of the statements that have been made have been exaggerated."

Representative Otis Pike was unwilling to let the Air Force off the hook so easily. When the USAF Comptroller, General Duward Crow, appeared, the same man who a year before had told the same committee there was no overrun in the C–5A, Pike attacked: "Didn't the Air Force know by the time of the hearings . . . last year that that $3.4 billion [the estimate for the total program] wasn't going to hold up in a million years?"

"On the basis of the information that I had at that time," said General Crow, "I thought it was a good estimate . . . Now these very large increases began to surface after our testimony over here last year."

Pike found this "incredible" and reminded General Crow that the House Military Operations Subcommittee had turned up copies of Air Force memos and documents showing that USAF officials had known about the overrun for several years without informing Congress about it. "What I'm concerned about is candor," Pike told the general, "and I don't think we get it."

Pike was particularly troubled by the haste with which the Air Force had exercised its option for Run B. Pike wanted to know why the option had to be exercised "before we have the slightest concept of what the first 58 [including the five test planes] are going to cost?" When an Air Force general explained, "this was a part of the contract," Pike could only express his amazement that the government had "exercised in January of this year [1969] an option to buy 57 additional aircraft, the price of which we will not know until 1971."

Pike had somehow heard a few details about a C–5A briefing in the office of Secretary Seamans during which Air Force officials proposed "spreading" or "reallocating" costs from Run A to Run B, "to avoid the appearance of excess profit for Run B aircraft." Pike confronted General Crow with this proposal and asked, "Isn't that really playing Mickey Mouse with the figures in order to avoid the appearance of a great profit?" General Crow denied this accusation, but conceded, "The language which attempted to explain how the adjustment takes place was probably unfortunate."

The language of the Air Force witnesses at the HASC hearing was generally more "fortunate," but not particularly informative. Some of this may have been due to the complexities of what was obviously a very complex contract, but much of it seemed intentionally designed to conceal or obscure the facts the committee was after. By using a 1964 estimate that was higher than the price listed in the contract, the Air Force managed to "reduce" the cost overrun. Even then, different Air Force witnesses cited overrun figures of $240 million, $382 million, and $670 million. As the Air Force continued its presentation, Representative William Dickinson (Rep.-Ala.) confessed, "the more I have gone into it the more confusing it is." For Representative Richard Ichord (Dem.-Mo.), there were "so many variables involved in here in making the computation, that the final figures, to say the least, are quite confusing to me."

Another major obstacle to the committee's understanding was the Air Force's habit of citing figures in piecemeal terms of annual budgets, instead of the total program figures the congressmen requested. At one point these tactics led Representative Samuel Stratton (Dem.-N.Y.) to explode, "I am not concerned about what you are required to budget. I am concerned about what the taxpayers are required to pay." General Thomas Jeffrey, an Air Force Deputy Chief of Staff, tried to explain the entire cost history of the C–5A program again, but added so little clarity to the discussion that Representative Stratton simply told him he was confusing everyone. General Jeffrey conceded the cost overrun was "an exceedingly complex question, and we feel it is very important that we make it clear for the record, and that the Committee thoroughly understand this very undesirable situation we find ourselves in."

In the hope of reducing the confusion, chairman Rivers invited the Air Force to come back the following week to make a full-scale presentation of the entire history of the C–5A program. This time the Air Force generals came armed with their slides, charts, and graphs, and this time they admitted to a cost overrun of $1.3 billion, including inflation and other "unforeseen difficulties" that the Total Package contract had supposedly foreseen. The generals did not include in this figure, however, spare parts and other "support" items. With these items included, the total program cost came to roughly $5.2 billion — the same figure that Fitzgerald had been citing and the Air Force emphatically denying for six months. Using this figure, the cost overrun came to $2 billion when compared to the original contract price.

General Jeffrey cautioned the committee to "avoid the use of the term overrun" in discussing the C–5A, and chairman Rivers agreed. Rivers warned his colleagues pointedly, "The people that used $2 billion overrun just plain don't know what they are talking about . . . These are not overruns, and anybody who calls them overruns is in error."

Chairman Rivers must have felt this settled the matter of the C-5A's cost overrun, but not Otis Pike. Pike could not understand how the Air Force could attribute $350 million of the cost overrun to the increased size of the C-5A. They had explained to the committee that the C-5A as constructed weighed about 40 tons more than the plane they had originally planned. But Pike wanted to know why the Air Force had not revised their cost estimates upward back in 1965, since Lockheed's contract proposal called for the larger plane. He could not believe the Air Force had only just learned that the increase in size would add $350 million to the cost of the plane. "I just find this incredible," exclaimed Pike. "I can't believe that the Air Force is that dumb. I choose to believe that it is a nice round number which was picked out of the hat to justify some of the overruns."

The Air Force version of the C-5A affair became even more incredible with the appearance before the committee of Ernest Fitzgerald, who had been invited to testify at the insistence of Pike and the other members of the Fearless Five. To the dismay of chairman Rivers, Fitzgerald clearly showed that the C-5A had indeed increased by $2 billion over the original contract price. On nearly every major point at issue during the hearings thus far, Fitzgerald contradicted the earlier Air Force testimony, using the Air Force's own figures. He disputed the official claim that attributed $500 million of the cost overrun to "abnormal inflation," showing that $300 million worth of inflation had been "built into" the original estimates. This left only $200 million that could really be called abnormal and therefore be considered part of the overrun.

Fitzgerald submitted a series of official memos and documents proving that the Air Force had known about the cost overrun on the C–5A since 1966. He showed how they had concealed part of this overrun from Congress by keeping the spare parts and other "support" items separate from their annual C–5A budget requests. The cost of these spares and other items alone, according to the documents that Fitzgerald produced, had tripled from an estimated $300 million in 1965, to nearly $1 billion in 1968. By leaving all of this out of the charts they had shown the committee, the Air Force had "reduced" the total cost of the entire program from $5.2 billion to $4.3 billion.

As Fitzgerald continued to demonstrate how the Air Force had concealed the C–5A cost overrun, Chairman Rivers grew increasingly nervous. At one point he cut in and asked Fitzgerald, "Do you think somebody in the Air Force is deliberately failing to give accurate figures on this contract?"

"No, sir," Fitzgerald replied. "I am making no such accusation at all."

"It looks kind of fishy to you," said Rivers, "but you don't accuse anybody of anything?"

"I have no basis for it, Mr. Chairman. No one has discussed with me the basis for selecting the estimate. I guess I would have to agree with your wording. It does look a little fishy."

Having failed in this attempt to goad Fitzgerald into open conflict with his superiors, Rivers tried another tack. Ignoring the fact that Fitzgerald had been working on the C–5A cost problems for three years, Rivers said, "It is remarkable to me how you have become right off the bat so knowledgeable on this thing . . . You became an expert pretty fast over there."

Fitzgerald said nothing.

Three weeks later, in June, when it resumed its hearings on the C–5A, the HASC called on the General Accounting Office to give

its report on the program. Since the GAO's investigators had
relied almost completely on the Air Force for their information,
their figures naturally matched those cited earlier by the Air
Force witnesses. The result was not particularly instructive. They
did not jibe with those cited by Fitzgerald, however, and a few
congressmen caught the discrepancy. As Representative Dickin-
son complained, "I notice we get several different answers at different times. I give up."

Otis Pike, however, refused to give up. He asked the GAO
about the accuracy of the current Air Force estimate for spare
parts. "Mr. Pike," a GAO staff man replied, "at the moment, I
don't think even the Air Force knows exactly how much they will
ultimately spend for spare parts for this aircraft." Pike pointed
out that while the contract called for Lockheed to provide spare
parts, it did not mention their price. In view of the soaring
estimates for the cost of spares, he found this appalling.

"I don't want to interrupt you," Rivers interrupted at this point,
"but there is no contract for spares."

"There is a contract that says they can't get them anywhere
else," Pike insisted.

"I don't care what the contract says!" Rivers shouted.

"Mr. Chairman, I do care what the contract says. I have seen
time after time in procurements, they get in trouble and so they
make up their hole by really laying it around on spare parts.
There's not a darned thing the Air Force can do about it . . .
Once they start to buy the equipment, they have got to have the
spare parts."

Pike was also upset by the clear evidence that the Air Force
had known about the overrun for the past few years without informing Congress about it. "We are asked to authorize and appropriate money based on one set of prices, which today you tell
us they should have known were wrong. We did authorize and

appropriate money, and now they say, 'Oh, you've got to go along with this because we started it, and you authorized the money.' We authorized the money based on bad statistics which they provided us with. I am deeply concerned about the question of fairness to Lockheed, but I am equally concerned about the question of fairness to the Congress and the taxpayers."

The following week former USAF Assistant Secretary Robert Charles appeared before the HASC and vehemently defended the contract he had created as "the toughest contract for a major defense system ever entered into by the Pentagon." He could not understand why he was being "portrayed as a giveaway artist, the gentleman with the golden handshake, the creator of the 'sweetheart' contract." The press, said Charles, had completely distorted the C-5A program. "Success has been pictured as failure, competition as negotiation, losses as undeserved profits. Superior technical achievement has been almost totally disregarded." He accused the plane's critics of "unwittingly performing a disservice to the taxpayer and to the national defense."

Charles challenged anyone to cite another Air Force program that could match the C-5A either in cost control or technical performance. He insisted that current flight tests indicated the plane would perform at "101 per cent" of its contract requirements. As for the cost problem, while conceding a "relatively small increase," he claimed the C-5A's cost history compared favorably with that of any other major weapon system. Most of them, said Charles, exceeded their original cost estimates by very wide margins, "often by several hundred per cent, and rarely below 100 per cent."

While Mr. Charles cited this comparison in praise of the C-5A, more critical observers might consider it a damnation of the entire defense procurement system. When a $2 billion cost overrun becomes "a relatively small increase," and compares "favorably" with the cost history of other major systems, something is drastically wrong.

Mendel Rivers, however, saw nothing wrong. Trying to cloak the C–5A in an aura of national urgency, he asked Charles if it constituted a "crash program."

"That is right," replied Charles, happy to have the protection of the term, although it was undoubtedly the first time anyone had used it to describe the C–5A program.

"Whenever you get in a crash program," said Rivers, "you can't help spending money."

"Precisely," Charles agreed.

Except for Congressmen Pike, Robert Leggett (Dem.-Cal.), and Charles Whalen (Rep.-Ohio), the other HASC members generally treated Charles kindly. Representative Charles Gubser (Rep.-Cal.) complimented him for "one of the most factual, forthright, sensible and logical statements I have ever heard. It is quite a contrast to some of the headline grabbing that has been going on."

Charles did give an impressive performance. He refused to concede any defects in the C–5A contract, and the committee considered this a noble stand. Congressman Durward Hall (Rep.-Mo.) particularly admired him for "sticking to his guns." Whenever Charles was confronted by apparent contradictions or conflicts in previous testimony, he managed to avoid the issue with charmingly evasive replies. For example, when Representative Leggett asked how the Air Force could estimate Lockheed's loss on the contract at $285 million when the company itself expected to almost break even, Charles simply replied, "Cost estimates are a pretty tricky thing. This is not an exact science."

Despite his generally cordial reception, Charles did have a few bad moments. At one point, after denying emphatically that the Air Force had allowed Lockheed to "buy-in" on the C–5A contract with an unreasonably low bid, he made one fascinating slip: "The cost overrun here is so much smaller as a percentage of what we expected it to be when we let the contract, that it is a great improvement." Upon close analysis, this remarkable statement confirms the charge that the Air Force did in fact accept a bid it knew was far too low and thus allowed Lockheed to buy in. Even more embarrassing, it clearly implies that when USAF officials sold the C–5A to Congress back in 1965 as a $3 billion program, they already "expected" costs to run considerably higher.

The following day Daniel Haughton and other Lockheed officials appeared before the HASC and received a warm welcome from chairman Rivers. After praising the company's achievement with previous military aircraft, Rivers lamented the way the company was being "lambasted in recent weeks by knowledgeable and unknowledgeable people, and a lot of people who ought to know better . . . It is ridiculous, the fine showing this plane has made. I understand — you can tell me — it has exceeded every expectation anybody in the know had of this plane. Is that a fact?"

Hardly the man to argue such a point, Mr. Haughton assured Rivers that the C–5A would surpass its performance requirements "by about seven per cent." Rivers, in turn, assured Haughton that the Air Force would definitely buy the entire 115-plane program. "Regardless of what this plane costs," said Rivers, "we need it, and we must have it."

Taking the cue from their leader, most of the other committee members lavished praise on the Lockheed officials. Representative John Hunt (Rep.-N.J.) told Haughton, "I think on the whole you have done an admirable job." Representative W. C. "Dan" Daniel (Dem.-Va.) commended them for "providing this effective weapon system for us." The cost increase on the C–5A did not seem to bother Representative Daniel. "Having just left the business world before coming to Congress," he could easily understand how "these things happen."

Even Congressman Floyd Hicks, from Boeing's home state of Washington, had nothing but praise for the C–5A and Lockheed. Hicks had just made a special visit to the Lockheed plant at Marietta and had apparently been treated royally by the company. The grateful Mr. Hicks told the Lockheed officials at the hearing, "the performance of your airplane is only exceeded by the hospitality that you show visiting firemen when they come down there." Mr. Hicks had no idea "whether these cost matters are responsibilities or things that you should be blamed for."

The committee's two Georgia congressmen were particularly impressed with a briefing and film on the C–5A presented by Lockheed-Georgia executives. "From this film," said Representative Jack Brinkley, "it appears to me we are getting our money's worth." (One might well wonder whether "we" referred to the Air Force, Congress, or Georgia.) Representative G. Elliott Hagan commended Mr. Haughton and Lockheed-Georgia president Thomas May for a "wonderful presentation" and "the wonderful job Lockheed has been doing." Despite the many obvious conflicts between the testimony of the Lockheed officials and the Air Force, Representative Hagan felt that the Lockheed officials had "certainly answered any question I could imagine this morning in their presentation."

If Georgia's Representative Hagan truly felt that all the questions about the C–5A affair had been settled by the Lockheed-Georgia presentation, one can only conclude that he had not been listening very carefully. For on almost every point of significance, except for the claims about the plane's performance, the Lockheed account conflicted sharply with that of the Air Force, as it had during the SASC hearings.

Even for those who had been listening, most of the figures that had been tossed around during the hearings were probably not worth much anyway, since they were already nearly one year old. Costs had obviously "grown" considerably during that year. Somehow the Air Force did not get around to updating its cost estimates on the C–5A program from October, 1968, just before the overrun was first exposed, until more than a year later, after Congress approved the funds for the fourth squadron. At the time of the HASC hearings, only a few planes had actually been built, with 22 others in various stages of construction.

Thus, when Otis Pike pressed General Crow on the October, 1968, estimates, he admitted they were developed "in a rather gross, crude way." The committee's able staff counsel, John Blandford, pointed out that "much of what we are discussing here . . . will never be known until sometime in 1973, when the program has been completed."

Chairman Rivers, for one, obviously did not care much about the cost estimates, whether they were accurate or not. He admonished the plane's critics for concentrating on its cost, instead of what he took to be its virtues. In the most lyrical moment of the HASC hearings, Rivers exclaimed, "This is a fantastic aircraft. It is the largest thing ever conceived by American industry. Who can imagine 750,000 pounds flying at over 550 miles an hour at 40,000 feet for 5000 miles? Of course we want to keep the costs down in every way humanly possible. But we've got to have this. It's as simple as that."

CHAPTER SEVEN
The Ordeal of Ernest Fitzgerald

"Cost reduction and cost control are by their very nature sort of anti-social activities."

Ernest Fitzgerald,
Deputy Assistant Secretary of the Air Force
for Management Systems

THOUGH BUSY DEFENDING ITSELF on Capitol Hill during the months of congressional hearings on the C–5A, the Pentagon also devoted a good deal of attention to the man it considered responsible for all this activity — Ernest Fitzgerald. When Senator Proxmire first informed the Air Force back in the fall of 1968 that he wished to call Fitzgerald as a witness, the new DoD Comptroller, Robert Moot, warned Fitzgerald that his testimony might "leave blood on the floor." [1]

At first the Pentagon refused to allow Fitzgerald to testify, but Proxmire insisted and finally wrote Fitzgerald a personal invitation. This letter was intercepted by the Air Force Office of Legislative Liaison. When asked about the interception of Proxmire's letter, the OLL claimed the action was part of a routine "screening process" applied to all official mail from congressmen to the Pentagon. They did not explain, however, how this process had picked up a personal letter. Fitzgerald finally received a copy of the original letter and soon afterward learned that high DoD officials were "disturbed" about his prospective testimony.

After more pressure from Proxmire, the Pentagon finally agreed to allow Fitzgerald to appear, but only as a "back-up witness" to George Bergquist, Deputy Assistant Secretary of Defense for Management Systems Development, implying that Fitzgerald was not competent to discuss the C–5A alone. The evening before the hearing Fitzgerald was called to a meeting at the Pentagon and informed that Bergquist would testify in his place. The next day at the hearing, however, Proxmire ignored Bergquist (who submitted a statement which shed no light on the C–5A) and called only upon Fitzgerald.

When he invited Fitzgerald to testify, in November, 1968, Proxmire asked him to bring a written statement breaking down the cost history of the C–5A. When Fitzgerald appeared before the subcommittee, however, he had no statement. Asked why, he said he had been forbidden to prepare one by "higher authorities." [2] Annoyed by this interference with his best witness, Proxmire demanded to know who had issued the order. No one in the Air Force seemed to know, or be willing to tell, although Assistant Secretary Robert Charles later admitted to having had an "indirect influence" on the decision. He told Proxmire that the C–5A was a "very complex matter" and that since Fitzgerald had no direct responsibility for procurement his discussion of the C–5A's cost problems "would not be placed in perspective." [3]

After a few inquiries the order was lifted, and Fitzgerald submitted the C–5A cost figures requested by Proxmire to his superiors for approval. Despite repeated queries from the subcommittee staff, however, the Air Force sat on this material for six weeks. By the time it finally arrived, it had suffered an accident similar to those which befell earlier unflattering reports on the C–5A. Labeled "Insert for the record/testimony of A. E. Fitzgerald," the estimates therein differed markedly from those Fitzgerald had actually made. The subcommittee sent the material back to the Pentagon and demanded Fitzgerald's own documents. These finally arrived on January 15, 1969, the day before Fitzgerald's next appearance before the subcommittee, and, more significantly, the day before the Air Force exercised its option for the second run of 57 more C–5As.[4]

When Proxmire wrote to Fitzgerald inviting him to appear at the January, 1969, hearing, the letter was intercepted again. This time, when it reached Fitzgerald's desk, it had been torn and stamped by the Office of Legislative Liaison. The envelope was missing, along with a document that had been in it when it left Proxmire's office. Just after the letter arrived, Fitzgerald received a phone call from a high DoD official who had obviously seen the letter, and who expressed displeasure about the idea of a second appearance by Fitzgerald before the Proxmire committee.

At the January, 1969, hearing, Fitzgerald not only confirmed his $2 billion overrun estimate, but pointed out that the reason his figures differed so much from those released by Air Force officials was that they had been omitting the cost of the C–5A's spare parts and other support expenses, which had grown from a 1965 estimate of $300 million to a current projection of nearly $1 billion. He also told the committee that in discussing the C–5A overrun, Air Force officials had for the first time been using a misleading 1964 figure as the original base estimate, rather than the actual lower contract target price of 1965.[5] The 1964 figure was a gross estimate for a so-called "parametric" airplane, the CXHLS — not the C–5A.

While Fitzgerald's disclosures impressed the Proxmire committee and caused a public furor, they hardly endeared him to his superiors at the Pentagon, and he soon began to encounter a series of mysterious "personnel" problems. Before learning about them, however, the reader should know a bit about his earlier career.

Reared in Birmingham, Alabama, during the Depression, Arthur Ernest Fitzgerald acquired a natural concern for thrift.

Upon graduation from the University of Alabama with a degree in industrial engineering, he worked as a quality control engineer for several large industrial companies, and then spent five years with the auditing firm of Arthur Young & Company as a management consultant to the firm's defense contractor clients. In 1962 he left Arthur Young to start his own consulting firm, Performance Technology Corporation. PTC received contracts from the Defense Department to study several large military programs, including the Minuteman Missile program, on which PTC turned up a huge cost overrun.

By 1965, when Fitzgerald was 38, his work on defense industry cost control had gained so much attention around the Pentagon that he was offered the $30,000 post of Deputy Assistant Secretary for Management Systems in the Air Force. Looking back now, he recalls accepting the job because he had become "increasingly concerned at the enormous waste that was evident in these programs . . . The large contractors appeared to have been told by the buying agencies of the Defense Department nor to worry about costs during the 'missile gap' days of the early 1960's . . . Consequently, overhead rates approximately doubled, and labor efficiency plummeted. In the factories of the contractors, labor efficiencies of only 20 to 50 per cent of normal industrial efficiencies became commonplace. In engineering and test operations, labor efficiency was generally even lower, with some organizations having little or no necessary work for long periods.

"In the absence of countervailing pressures from the Government, average overall wages and salaries in Air Force ballistic missile work increased approximately 50 per cent between 1960 and 1965. In the permissive atmosphere of those free-spending days, cost controls in the operations of big weapons contractors, which were never strong, practically collapsed. To compound the problem, [this] was accompanied by more permissive attitudes in technical areas, and weapon performance and quality suffered accordingly.

"The attraction of this new job for me was to see whether the attitudes I saw in the field — the prime cause of the problem — could be corrected from above. It was clear to me that nothing could be done with the field. I had hoped that once inside the Pentagon, I could identify dramatic opportunities for cost reductions. I felt that if I could make this clear to the people at the top, something would be done about it. I was wrong." [6]

In September, 1965, ten days before the C–5A contract was signed, Fitzgerald came to the Pentagon. His job gave him a roving charter to examine and recommend ways of cutting costs on all major Air Force programs, including the C–5A. In the beginning, things went well, for he seemed to have the backing of the top officials in DoD. "Any time we could bring a major issue to the attention of Defense Secretary McNamara or Under Secretary [Paul] Nitze, we could get a favorable ruling." But as the Vietnam war began to take up more of McNamara's time and attention, the pressure for cost control diminished, and, according to Fitzgerald, there was no longer any "followthrough." Nevertheless, by 1967 his own efforts had earned him the Air Force's nomination for the Defense Department Distinguished Civilian Service Award, a fact the Air Force must now find somewhat embarrassing.

After his testimony before the Proxmire committee, Fitzgerald received no further awards, but the Air Force certainly gave his career considerable attention. In September, 1968, two months before his first appearance on Capitol Hill, Fitzgerald had received official notice — signed by the chief of the DoD civilian personnel division — that his position would henceforth be protected by Civil Service regulations, a normal tenure earned by his three years in the job. Twelve days after his testimony to Proxmire, however, he was stripped of this protection. The Air Force personnel office claimed there had been an unfortunate "computer error" — the first such error the computer had made in 1600 personnel actions during the past 18 months. Air Force Secretary Harold Brown assured Proxmire this 1600-to-1 shot was in no way related to Fitzgerald's recent testimony.

In January, 1969, Proxmire got hold of a Pentagon memo prepared at the request of Secretary Brown, listing three possible ways to get rid of Fitzgerald: outright discharge for misconduct, a "reduction in force" that would simply abolish his job, and a complex third method which, according to the memo, while perfectly legal, would also be "rather underhanded, and probably not be approved by the Civil Service Commission." When questioned by Proxmire about this memo, Robert Charles insisted it merely outlined "various things that could happen under certain conditions," although he did concede that the memo's wording "may have been unfortunate." Proxmire told Charles, "If I were working for anybody, and a memorandum like this was written on how you could handle me, and get rid of me, I would figure that they were not exactly contemplating a promotion, or giving me a medal." [7]

Despite all the interest in arranging for his departure, Fitzgerald managed to stay on at the Pentagon, undoubtedly due in large part to the publicity his case was receiving in the press and the diligence with which Proxmire pursued it. Among his colleagues, who obviously recognized a pariah when they saw one, Fitzgerald encountered "a general cooling of relationships." The chill did not bother the amiable Alabaman much, for as his wife says, "He's the kind of guy who can take this sort of thing." Fitzgerald did take it and somehow managed to remain fairly cheerful. "Cost reduction and cost control," he says, "are by their very nature sort of anti-social activities. Nobody really likes the efficiency expert, and I think that a good one expects that, and doesn't try to win any popularity contests."

Unwilling to simply fire Fitzgerald, the Air Force managed to restrict his activity in a manner worthy of Kafka. Soon after his testimony in January, 1969, he was removed from contact with all major Air Force programs, and specifically from the C–5A. He was no longer invited to top-level USAF briefings on program management and no longer received copies of routine program reports and cost data. One of his two assistants was transferred, and the other was instructed to report only to Fitzgerald's superior. In March, cost control authority for the C–5A was officially transferred from his Office of Financial Management to the USAF Systems Command, the very organization that had allowed the C–5A costs to get out of control and then concealed them. Fitzgerald then received a new project list, comprised of such relative trivia as the construction of a 20-lane bowling alley in Thailand. Characteristically, his first action was to question the need for the bowling alley.

While the Air Force thus removed Fitzgerald from any further contact with potentially embarrassing information, it could not control his extracurricular activities. During that spring of 1969, with plenty of extra time on his hands, Fitzgerald began working closely in his evenings with a small group of legislative staff aides, including Richard Kaufman and Peter Stockton, who had organized a weekly seminar for their colleagues on military procurement. One purpose of the seminars was to help them draft amendments to the 1970 military procurement bill that would help bring military spending under congressional control.

The Pentagon soon learned about Fitzgerald's work on Capitol Hill. When Air Force Secretary Seamans appeared before a closed session of the House Armed Services Committee in May, he complained about it, but hedged, "I am not saying this is wrong, mind you."

"If it isn't wrong," asked Representative Otis Pike, "why is it pertinent?"

"It is very interesting," replied Seamans, "that in the testimony in front of a number of committees, documents keep appearing, some of which are confidential, that were obtained from Mr. Fitzgerald."

HASC Chairman Rivers then told Seamans, "If I had a fellow like that in my office, he would have been long gone. You don't need to be afraid about firing him." [8] Coming from Rivers, this remark clearly indicated that the Air Force would not have to worry about congressional reaction if it fired Fitzgerald. In fact, Rivers later took the trouble to announce to the press that on the basis of what Seamans had told the committee about Fitzgerald's leaking of classified information, he, Rivers, felt Fitzgerald should definitely be fired.

While leaking classified documents certainly represents sufficiently serious grounds to fire a Pentagon employee, Seamans' charge had one slight flaw — it was not true. When the HASC released the record of its hearings in September, 1969, and the accusation was made public, Fitzgerald immediately denied the charge, calling it a "smear" which could seriously damage his career. (By then he realized he would soon be returning to his industrial consulting work.) "It is entirely possible," he said, "for completely unfounded accusations to be placed in my security record, which could result in doors being closed, particularly if you are working in any company that deals with the government." In September, and again in October, Fitzgerald formally requested an opportunity to discuss the charges against him with Seamans. In neither case did he even receive the courtesy of a reply. When Seamans appeared before the Proxmire subcommittee the following November, the senator challenged him to substantiate his accusation, and Seamans backed down — six months after the damage had been done.

In June, 1969, when Fitzgerald was scheduled to appear again before the Proxmire subcommittee, he received a memo 15 minutes before the hearing opened, forbidding him to testify on the C–5A. Proxmire accused the Air Force of "blatant muzzling" of a congressional witness and wrote an angry note to Secretary of Defense Melvin Laird. That evening he was informed that Fitzgerald was "free" to testify after all. When he appeared, Proxmire asked him to submit additional written information on the C–5A for the hearing record. However, since Fitzgerald had been relieved of responsibility for the C–5A, he no longer had access to current cost data and had to request it through official channels. His superiors refused, suggesting that Proxmire contact the office of the Secretary of the Air Force directly for the information.

After his June appearance before the Proxmire subcommittee, Fitzgerald was invited to another hearing, this time a private one with Secretary Laird, which Fitzgerald described as a "get-acquainted meeting." There was no discussion of any changes in his job status, but as Fitzgerald commented afterward, "Something will have to happen soon." It did. Five months later, when the C–5A was no longer in the news, the Air Force "restructured" its Office of Financial Management as part of an "economy move" and eliminated the position of Deputy for Management Systems, giving Fitzgerald two months' notice. USAF Secretary Seamans insisted that Fitzgerald had not been "fired." It was simply a matter of being unable to find "a suitable new position in which he could make a contribution." In private conversations with various congressmen, however, Seamans and other USAF officials gave other reasons for Fitzgerald's dismissal. In addition to the charge of leaking classified material, Fitzgerald was accused of not being a "team player." [9]

Despite these private explanations, 60 members of the House were sufficiently appalled by Fitzgerald's dismissal to write a joint letter of protest to President Nixon. "Honesty and candor,"

they wrote, "exhibited by public servants without fear of reprisal
must remain a keystone of good government. Therefore we call
upon the Administration to repudiate the type of action that was
taken against Mr. Fitzgerald, and restore him to his former
duties." The only response to this protest came from a Deputy
Assistant to the President, who assured them that their "concern"
would be "called to the President's attention at the earliest opportunity." [10]

To Fitzgerald and those who had followed his career since his
first disclosure of the C—5A overrun a year before, the final blow
came as no surprise. Given the authoritarian structure of the
Pentagon, once he spoke out publicly he effectively ended his
career there, and he probably realized that himself. From that
point on, however well protected he was on the Hill, his dismissal
was only a matter of time, if the Air Force's ham-handed harass-
ment did not make him quit first. In the matter of timing, the Air
Force acted with some skill, waiting until the public furor had
died down and Congress had approved additional funds for the
C—5A. The actual firing, however, lacked style. Surely the Pentagon's public relations men could have come up with a less embar-
rassingly ironic excuse for sacking Fitzgerald than an "economy
move."

Shortly after the Pentagon announced Fitzgerald's dismissal in
November, Proxmire called a hearing to compel the Air Force to
explain its grounds for the move. After demolishing the charge
of security violations, he pointedly asked Seamans several times
if the Air Force had conducted an investigation of Fitzgerald
in order to dig up grounds for firing him. On six separate
occasions, Seamans, who was not under oath, replied no. He
told Proxmire, "I can say categorically that such an investigation
would never take place without my approval, and it could not
take place without it." [11] He did admit that the Air Force Office

of Special Investigations had opened a "routine informational file" on Fitzgerald because he was "newsworthy." He said the file contained only newspaper clippings and the like.

Curious about this "routine" file, Military Operations Subcommittee member William Moorhead later questioned Brigadier General Joseph Cappucci, Director of the USAF Office of Special Investigations. General Cappucci admitted that his agents had questioned several military and civilian informants in search of unfavorable information on Fitzgerald. (Fitzgerald himself says that about the same time a retired officer employed by a major defense contractor had also been asking his friends about his drinking habits and sex life.) When Representative Moorhead confronted Secretary Seamans with this obvious contradiction to his testimony before the subcommittee, Seamans claimed the OSI's search was merely a "special inquiry" and did not constitute an investigation. Moorhead disagreed: "I am bothered by the Air Force's peculiar semantic distinction between a 'special inquiry' and 'investigation.' I cannot see any difference. I am disturbed that this was not a passive effort in which the Air Force simply received information, but an active effort by the Office of Special Investigations to seek out persons hostile to Mr. Fitzgerald." [12]

Pressed by Moorhead and Proxmire, the Air Force agreed to show them the contents of the OSI file on Fitzgerald. When Lieutenant Colonel Clifford LaPlante, of the USAF Office of Legislative Liaison, brought the file to Proxmire's office, he found Proxmire, Moorhead, their staff aides, and Fitzgerald waiting. Acting upon orders from Seamans, Lieutenant Colonel LaPlante said that only Proxmire and Moorhead could see the file.

"Certainly Mr. Fitzgerald can see his own file," Proxmire protested.

"It's not his file," said LaPlante.

When Fitzgerald asked why he could not see it, LaPlante

replied, "It's just not our policy." So, Fitzgerald and the staff aides left the room, and Proxmire and Moorhead went through the file. They found in it frivolous statements from anonymous informants identified only as "T-1, T-2," etc. One accused Fitzgerald of being a "penny pincher" because he drove an old Rambler. Another said he was "overbearing" about saving money on defense contracts — which was precisely his job.

Having gone through the file, Proxmire returned it to Lieutenant Colonel LaPlante, assuming it had been complete. He should have known better, considering his earlier experiences with Air Force documents relating to the C—5A affair. A few days later he learned that the Air Force had removed certain items from the file before showing it to him. One report purposely omitted described an interview with former Assistant Secretary Leonard Marks, Fitzgerald's ex-boss in the Office of Financial Management. In the interview, Marks had praised Fitzgerald for his loyalty and dedication and told the USAF investigator: "You go back to your boss [General Cappucci] and tell him that Ted Marks says you're on a wild goose chase. If this gets out it's only going to hurt the Air Force." When reporters tried to learn why this statement had been omitted from the file, an Air Force spokesman said the interview with Marks was not an interview, but "simply checking." [13]

The same day the Air Force announced the elimination of Fitzgerald's job, the new Assistant Secretary for Financial Management, Spencer Schedler (a former advance man for Vice President Spiro Agnew's 1968 campaign), hired an accountant named John Dyment as a consultant on cost controls for major Air Force contracts. Though the official description of his duties sounded quite similar to those of Fitzgerald's old job, the Air Force denied that Dyment had been hired to replace Fitzgerald. A former classmate of Assistant Secretary Schedler at Harvard

Business School, Dyment is a partner in the accounting firm of Arthur Young & Company for which Schedler's wife works as an auditor. One of Arthur Young & Company's biggest clients happens to be Lockheed Aircraft. Since the Air Force's biggest financial problem at the time was Lockheed's C–5A, the hiring of a partner of Lockheed's accounting firm as a consultant to the USAF Office of Financial Management brought a round of criticism from the press and Congress. Proxmire called it "a shocking conflict-of-interest." Representative Moorhead compared it to "sending a bulldog to guard the hamburger."

The Air Force tried to play down the conflict story, pointing out that Dyment worked in Arthur Young's New York management services division, not the Los Angeles auditing division which handles the Lockheed account. Assistant Secretary Schedler saw no conflict-of-interest in the Dyment appointment, insisting he had taken a "straight-arrow approach" in the matter. Dyment himself saw no potential conflict in his work for the Air Force. He claimed that at $100 a day, he would be working for only a quarter of his normal consulting fee, because he felt companies such as his have "a responsibility to make this contribution" to the government. Despite all these disclaimers, criticism of the appointment continued. The Air Force finally decided it could get along without Mr. Dyment's contribution and quietly dropped him after only one day on the job.

With the air already full of investigations, Proxmire called on the Justice Department to conduct one into the firing of Fitzgerald, citing a federal law (Title 18, Section 1505 of the U.S. Criminal Code) which classifies as a criminal offense, punishable by up to five years in prison, "any attempt to threaten, influence, intimidate, or impede" any witness in connection with a congressional investigation or to "injure" any witness for testimony to Congress.

At a press conference following the November, 1969, hearings of his subcommittee, Proxmire recounted the entire Fitzgerald affair and concluded: "Now we know a crime has been committed. The provisions of this statute have been clearly violated. We know the victim is Ernest Fitzgerald, and we know an attempt was made to obstruct a Congressional hearing. It is therefore the duty of the Department of Justice to identify the perpetrators of the criminal acts and to take the necessary actions against them, whoever they may be . . . The law has been violated . . . The law should be enforced."

Quoting from a letter he had written to Attorney General Mitchell, Proxmire raised the question of "whether there is law and order in the Department of Defense. . . . I believe the Federal Government is on trial over the handling of the Fitzgerald affair."

Assistant Attorney General Will Wilson, head of the Justice Department's Criminal Division, assured Proxmire the Fitzgerald case would receive "priority treatment." After more than a year of priority treatment, and without bothering to interview Fitzgerald himself, the Justice Department decided to take no action.

Meanwhile, Fitzgerald himself, with the help of the American Civil Liberties Union, has appealed his dismissal to the U.S. Civil Service Commission. If that fails, he plans to bring suit in federal court to force his reinstatement. "I won't give up on this," he told reporters. "I plan to give them hell." The ACLU charged that the Pentagon's "reprisals" against Fitzgerald "affect not only his own right of free speech; they create a climate of fear which will drive honest men out of government."

Assuming the Fitzgerald affair was actually brought to President Nixon's attention, he might well have recalled a speech he had made on April 26, 1951, denouncing the Truman administration for harassing congressional witnesses. Senator Nixon proposed a bill calling for five years in prison for any government official who retaliated against a subordinate because of his testimony before a congressional committee. "It is essential to the security of the nation," said Senator Nixon in support of his bill, "that every witness have complete freedom from reprisal when he is given an opportunity to tell what he knows." [15]

CHAPTER EIGHT

The Whittaker Report and Other Ploys

"There was really not sufficient visibility — both performance-wise and cost-wise."

Robert Seamans,
Secretary of the Air Force

DESPITE THE EFFORTS of Mendel Rivers, the C–5A hearings on Capitol Hill produced enough damaging publicity to worry the new regime across the river at the Pentagon. Like any good military organization finding itself under attack, the Pentagon counterattacked with the traditional weapons of bureaucracy. Defense Secretary Laird tried to pass the whole C–5A scandal off as a product of the Johnson-McNamara era. In April, 1969, when Representative Moorhead forced the Air Force to admit its concealment of the C–5A cost overrun, Laird issued a press release declaring that in the future, "full and accurate information on the C–5A and all other procurement matters" would be "promptly" given to Congress and the public. In a memorandum circulated within the Pentagon, and released to the press, he set forth his principles on public information: "No information will be classified solely because disclosure might result in criticism of the Department of Defense." [1]

While public declarations such as these made good copy for Pentagon press releases, Laird sounded somewhat less concerned about the public's right to know in certain documents of more limited circulation. In a confidential memo to three top civilian aides, Laird complained about "the allusions in the press and elsewhere to 'runaway' costs on such key or major programs as the C–5." He asked for reports in five days on "What sorts of actions on DoD's part can be taken to thwart or ameliorate the continuing adverse commentary on program costs and suspect technical effectiveness." [2]

To an outsider, the most obvious way to cut down on the criticism of runaway costs would seem to be to cut down on runaway costs. To the Pentagon, however, the obvious way to counteract unpleasant publicity on any major program is to get rid of the people most closely associated with it. On April 30, 1969, Secretary Laird called a press conference to say he was "very concerned" about the C–5A and promised a "full-scale review" of the entire program. He also announced the departure of Robert Charles and Fitzgerald's boss, Thomas Nielson. (Neilson had replaced Leonard Marks in 1967 as Assistant Secretary of the Air Force for Financial Management.) While men in such positions are often replaced by incoming administrations, and a DoD press release specifically denied that this "personnel action" had anything to do with the C–5A affair, the meaning of their departure was quite clear to most Pentagon officials.

In his farewell press conference on May 2, Charles defended the C–5A contract as "the best ever entered into by the Air Force." The new administration, he insisted, "has inherited a hell of a good program." [3] The new administration, however, did not seem to share this opinion. In a statement issued later that day, Secretary Laird pointedly refrained from endorsing Mr. Charles' handling of the C–5A program. According to Daniel Henkin, DoD's Assistant Secretary for Public Affairs, Laird had seen a draft of the Charles statement and had told him he "had no objection" to its release. Charles told reporters he "assumed" this meant Laird agreed with his statement, but Henkin made sure no

newsmen got that impression. Referring to Charles' claim that the
C–5A represented "a hell of a good program," Henkin said only
that "Mr. Laird certainly hopes this proves to be the case." [4]

In addition to holding press conferences and replacing token
officials, the Pentagon's standard response to bad publicity usually
includes the creation of a "high-level review." Reviews serve two
extremely useful purposes apart from their announced goals.
They give the impression of official concern, and, depending on
their duration, they provide an excellent escape from embarrassing
questions. The Air Force C–5A Program Review, headed by
Assistant Secretary Philip Whittaker, who had replaced Charles,
enabled harried DoD officials to avoid or parry queries from both
Armed Services Committees and inquisitive newsmen during the
spring and summer of 1969.

Whittaker told the Senate Armed Services Committee in June
that his review would be conducted "on a completely open, objec-
tive and impartial basis" and later described it to the press as
"neither a whitewash nor a witchhunt." His review team consisted of 11 different panels with 35 full-time Air Force specialists,
and additional part-time men. Though not previously connected
with the C–5A program, these Air Force personnel were all drawn
from the commands responsible for it. The fact that they had not
had any direct relation to the program was supposed to insure
their objectivity, but it also meant they had to rely on the men
close to the program for much of their information — the same
men who for years had been ignoring, concealing, or distorting
reports on the C–5A.

In preparing his report, Whittaker also drew on a concurrent
study of Lockheed's management and production methods di-
rected by the Air Force Chief of Staff, General McConnell. He
then presented his findings to "an outside group of distinguished
citizens of varied backgrounds": two NASA officials, a professor

of accounting, and an IBM executive. Though these four were undoubtedly men of good will, they knew nothing of the C–5A program and had to rely on the findings of the review team for their own education. About the only authority Whittaker did not consult at length was Fitzgerald, his Deputy Assistant Secretary for Management Systems, and the only official likely to offer an informed and critical analysis of the C–5A program. His session with Fitzgerald took all of ten minutes.

The Whittaker Report was due around the end of June, but the Air Force did not release it until a month later, which left sufficient time for judicious editing. At a press conference on July 28, 1969, Air Force Secretary Seamans released a summary of the report.[5] Though it mentioned a number of what he termed "deficiencies and ambiguities" in the C–5A contract, Seamans considered the report generally favorable and said it would be used as a "basis for moving ahead with the program." Besides, he added, in a remark which showed just how much influence the review had actually had on his decision, there is simply "no real alternative currently available."

The Whittaker Report claimed that costs on the entire C–5A program, including engines and spare parts, had risen from an "original" estimate of $3.4 billion to a projected cost of $5.1 billion — a 50 per cent increase. The trouble with these figures is that the Air Force was still trying to pass off its own arbitrary (and in this context meaningless) 1964 estimates as "original," instead of the actual figures in the 1965 contract, which were nearly half a billion dollars lower. The effect was to "cut" the cost overrun for popular consumption by $500 million.

Probably realizing that even its current estimate of $5.1 billion for the entire program was an optimistic figure, the report raised "the distinct possibility" that costs might continue to rise. Nevertheless, the report still mustered enough enthusiasm to conclude that "the C–5A will be a good buy even at the substantially increased costs." One can only wonder at what astronomical price the Air Force would no longer consider the C–5A "a good buy."

When reporters asked whether the huge overrun meant the Air Force had allowed Lockheed to "buy-in" at an unrealistically low price, Whittaker declared there was "no evidence of a buy-in as far as we can determine." The report termed the Lockheed bid merely "overly optimistic." Later in the conference, however, Whittaker admitted that Lockheed may have formulated its low bid on the C–5A with the prospect of profits on a commercial version in mind. When one reporter suggested such a bid would in fact constitute a "buy-in," Whittaker hedged, claiming it all depends on how "buy-in" is defined.

As for the repricing formula, which critics charged would enable Lockheed to more than make up any losses resulting from the buy-in, the report termed it "well-intentioned, but poorly structured, and not fully comprehended at the time of the award." This same delicate tone of understatement ran through the Whittaker Report, which concluded, "On balance, the overall job of managing the C–5A program . . . seems to have been underestimated by the Air Force." [6] Summing up the lessons learned from the C–5A affair, Secretary Seamans said, "The mistake, if you want to call it a mistake, is that there was not really sufficient visibility — both performance-wise and cost-wise."

For the Air Force, Lockheed, and others with a stake in the C–5A, the controversy over its cost came at an awkward time — just as the annual military procurement bill, by now completed and reported out by the Armed Services Committees, approached debate and vote by Congress. Both Senate and House approval would be needed to keep the $533 million C–5A authorization intact, and several congressmen had already announced their intention to try to block these funds for the fourth squadron. In view of Lockheed's well-publicized financial difficulties with the

C–5A, some wags on Capitol Hill had already dubbed the C–5A authorization "The Lockheed Relief Bill."

To counteract this unpleasant publicity, and improve the plane's public image, the Air Force and Lockheed PR men cranked out dozens of press releases hailing the plane's alleged capabilities. The Air Force Public Affairs Office, with a 1969 budget of $9.5 million, was well equipped for this job of image-building. It produced a 30-minute feature film entitled *C–5 Galaxy, World's Largest Aircraft,* which its film libraries at Air Force bases around the country offered to loan out to local clubs. Under its Distinguished Visitor Program, the Air Force PAO flew groups of influential community leaders from around the country down to the Lockheed-Georgia plant at Marietta for a briefing on the C–5A and its importance to the nation's security. Other strategic stops on this VIP tour included Florida, Hawaii, and Las Vegas.

Meanwhile the threat of a cutback in production had sent shivers through Georgia's Cobb County, and local officials made sure their congressmen were aware of what the C–5A meant to the economy of the area. The most graphic illustration of its importance occurred each week when an Air Force disbursing officer stationed at the Marietta plant handed a Lockheed official a check for $10 million or so as "progress payment." While much of that money flowed to out-of-state subcontractors, a good deal of it stayed right at home in Georgia. About $4 million each week paid the salaries of 26,000 employees at the Marietta plant, who then spent the money mostly in Cobb and other nearby counties. Each payroll dollar turned over an average of seven times, providing the lifeblood of the local economy. As a result of this transfusion, retail sales had boomed in that part of Georgia and Cobb County real estate had doubled in value since Lockheed won the C–5A contract.

Georgia congressmen were not the only ones to receive messages of support for the C–5A from influential constituents. In addition to Lockheed-Georgia's own sub-assembly plants in South Carolina, Tennessee, West Virginia, Pennsylvania, and Ohio, the parent Lockheed Aircraft Corporation has plants in 20 other states. The C–5A's 2000 subcontractors in 41 states also stood to suffer from any cutback in the program. In Palos Verdes, California, workers at Northrop Electronics were constructing the C–5A's navigation system. In Bloomfield, Connecticut, Kaman Aircraft was turning out the Galaxy's wing flaps. The plane's flight control system was being built by Honeywell in Minneapolis, Minnesota, and its wheels, tires, and brakes by B. F. Goodrich in Troy, Ohio. Bendix Corporation's aerospace division in South Bend, Indiana, had the subcontract for the C–5A's landing gear. Brunswick Corporation had the radar system, at its Marion, Virginia, plant.[7]

Most of these major subcontracts were multimillion dollar deals, which made them as vital to their communities as Lockheed-Georgia is to Marietta and Georgia. In Nashville, Tennessee, for example, AVCO's $125 million subcontract for the C–5A's wings made it the largest industrial project in Nashville history. In one way or another, most of these companies contribute heavily to the election campaigns of their congressmen, and it would not be surprising if their generosity was frequently called to the legislators' attention as the vote on the C–5A authorization drew near. In addition to their contributions, these firms probably reminded their congressmen of the 125,000 men employed on the C–5A program. As the congressmen well know, these men and their families vote, and they might think unkindly at election time of any senator or representative so misguided as to oppose the project responsible for their weekly paychecks.

CHAPTER NINE

The Great Senate Debate

*"For the first time in my memory, Congress can do
something about an overrun before it is too late. If we
fail to act, we have only ourselves to blame."*

Senator William Proxmire
in a Senate speech, September 3, 1969

ANYONE READING the papers in 1969 would have thought the
time propitious for an attack on the C–5A, for the air was filled
with criticism of defense spending, most of it centered on the
Anti-Ballistic Missile system. For the first time, a coalition of
citizens' organizations and congressmen had formed a concerted
effort to cut some of the more blatant examples of military waste
out of the procurement bill. As in any battle, however, timing
and strategy are vital to legislative success, and the amateur
coalition proved no match in such matters for the professionals
who managed the bill through both houses of Congress.

After the bruising summer battle over the ABM, won by its
proponents by a single vote, the Senate adjourned for a three-week
recess to allow members to lick their wounds in the hinterlands
and escape the capital's sticky August heat. When the Senate
reconvened in September to take up the C–5A and other items
on the Pentagon's shopping list, the citizens' coalition had lost
most of its energy. In an article in *The Nation*, Proxmire's subcommittee aide, Richard Kaufman, described this problem:

Unfortunately that coalition turned out to be too ephemeral to sus-
tain its pressure during the debate over military spending that

followed the ABM vote. The steady stream up Capitol Hill of citizens' groups, emissaries from the universities, ex-officials and statesmen who indefatigably buttonholed their Congressmen and Senators to argue the case against the ABM, who held conferences, wrote papers, reports and speeches, conducted press conferences, and took out ads in major dailies, slowed to a trickle after that first August vote. When the debate resumed in September, it had dried up almost completely.[1]

Although the C−5A's critics lacked the popular support that the anti-ABM movement had received, they did get one major break. A few days before debate on the C−5A opened, a fascinating story by Bernard Nossiter appeared in the *Washington Post,* revealing a hitherto classified report by the Pentagon's Office of Systems Analysis on the need for a fourth squadron of C−5As.[2] (Proxmire had been trying to obtain this report from the Air Force for several weeks, in vain.) Entitled "Major Program Memorandum for Strategic Mobility Forces," the June, 1969, report analyzed projected force levels over the next five years and concluded that three squadrons (58 planes) of C−5As plus other air and sea transport would be sufficient to meet America's future strategic contingencies.

The OSA report stated that the enormous cost of buying and operating the C−5As could only be justified if they were used in the first ten days of a conflict. Thereafter the smaller C−141s and ocean freighters could do the job more cheaply. The Army, according to this paper, could simply not mobilize its troops and equipment fast enough to fill more than three squadrons of C−5As plus the existing C−141s in ten days. In other words, if the Pentagon bought and operated ships with the same funds it proposed to spend on C−5As, the ships would do the same job for much less money. At equal cost for construction and operation, over a period of 20 days ships could carry twice as much cargo to Europe as C−5As. Over 50 days, the capacity of the ships becomes five times as great. Since the vast majority of military cargo is carried in peacetime or in situations such as Vietnam, when the element of time in terms of days is not crucial, the C–5A would only become worth its bloated price in times of emergency. The Systems Analysis report also found that because of its escalated cost, the C–5A was no longer an economical replacement for the C–141 in terms of cost per ton-mile, despite its larger cargo capacity. For all these reasons, the OSA report concluded that a fourth squadron of C–5As would "exceed" the Defense Department's requirements. In other words, they were not needed.

In contrast to this Systems Analysis report, which the Pentagon had immediately classified and buried, DoD officials had been telling the Armed Services Committees that they had to have the fourth squadron of C–5As and that the planes would bring a great savings over existing costs for cargo transport. The committees' members had been convinced by the Pentagon's claims and were not about to be dissuaded by any Systems Analysis cost studies or the *Washington Post,* which HASC chairman Rivers once described in a committee hearing as "not worth a damn." [3] Their main concern was an amendment submitted by Senator Proxmire that would delete the $533 million for the 23 planes of the proposed fourth squadron. The amendment would also limit the program to the 58 planes already authorized by Congress until the General Accounting Office completed a 90-day review of the cost and necessity of the C–5A program.

On Wednesday, September 3, 1969, the United States Senate took up the C–5A affair.[4] Those who missed the debate that day may appreciate its flavor more by learning that just prior to consideration of the Proxmire amendment, that august body was occupied by Senator Strom Thurmond's speech in praise of the Aiken, South Carolina, Pony League All-Stars, who had just competed in the Pony League World Series.

Senator Stennis, as floor leader for the entire $20 billion

military procurement authorization bill, led off with an attack on the Proxmire and other amendments aimed at cutting defense spending. He claimed they would "cut the bone and muscle out of our 1975 military capability." Raising the specter of an utterly defenseless nation, Stennis warned, "if these weaponry amendments are passed . . . the safety of the American people will be placed in jeopardy." In case anyone mistook his remarks for a slur on anyone's patriotism, he assured the Senate that he did not "challenge the motives of the authors of the amendments: I do seriously challenge their judgment." He claimed the amendments would reduce America to "a second-rate nation by 1975 . . . second best to the Russians in the years ahead," and unprepared for any "future D-Day."

Senator Proxmire scoffed at the idea that his amendment would in any way jeopardize the nation's security. "The C-5A has little if anything to do with the real defense of this nation," he insisted. "Rapid deployment has been defended as a part of a long-range policy . . . but this policy has not yet been adopted . . . The argument that a 90-day delay in the authorization of a fourth squadron of C-5A's in any way endangers the defense program is plainly ridiculous."

When Stennis came to the C-5A itself, he admitted he did not like the contract, but since it existed he saw no reason to cut back on it now. He agreed that costs on the program had risen, but assured everyone the plane was meeting all its performance requirements. As evidence of his concern, Stennis mentioned that he had inspected the plane itself when it flew up for a recent air show at Washington's Dulles International Airport. His inspection, however, had been somewhat limited: "It was the first time I have ever been to a big air show. I went out there to go through the C-5A. All I could see was the outside. However, other Senators will speak here who know what is inside the plane, and what is in the motor."

Stennis then brought up the matter of the Systems Analysis Report and countered it with a letter from Secretary Laird. In his letter Laird urged approval of the fourth squadron as essential to national defense and claimed that the Assistant Secretary for Systems Analysis, after a "reevaluation" (requested by Laird), now supported Laird's position. Proxmire belittled this sudden conversion. "I would expect nothing else," he said. "After all, he is in the chain of command. The Defense Department has to be monolithic in this. Once the Secretary of Defense and the other top officials have made this decision, I would expect them all to agree with it."

Later in the debate Senator George Murphy disputed the Systems Analysis report by pointing out that its conclusions did not match "the testimony that we had in the Armed Services Committee. This item would not be included in the bill if that were the case." He clearly implied that the rest of the Senate should accept the views of its Armed Services Committee. Proxmire strongly disagreed. "I have a lot of faith in the Armed Services Committee," he said. "I think it is a great committee. I agree that they did spend a lot of time and did listen to a great deal of testimony. However, I think it is a serious mistake for Senators to accept the recommendations of any committee carte blanche when the recommendations amount to billions and billions of dollars. It is our responsibility to challenge and debate the issues on the floor, and on appropriate occasions to disagree with the Committee. I think that too rarely in the past have we done this."

Senator Barry Goldwater then took the floor to present the Senate Armed Services Committee's main argument for the C–5A. He gave a long and complicated analysis of the contract, the overrun, and other aspects of the C–5A that often followed word for word the testimony given by the Air Force before the SASC. This is not surprising, for the Pentagon often "assists" loyal congressmen in the preparation of their speeches in defense of

particular military programs. Goldwater's loyalty to the military
has never been questioned. It frequently enables him to brush
aside any evidence that conflicts with his point of view. "I may be
wrong," he now told his fellow senators, "but I think I am right.
I think one must take into consideration what the military advisors
ask for. With respect to cost-effectiveness, perhaps the whole airplane is wrong, but it is the only thing we have in this field. It
is something the Chiefs [Joint Chiefs of Staff] have asked for, and
it has been sent down here by the President in his message . . .
it has been requested by the military, and we must pay attention
to what they want."

Senator Stennis tried to warn that if Congress cut the funds
for the fourth squadron, Lockheed might not be able to complete
production on the first 58 planes, because it had already spent
much more on them than the contract provided for. Senator
Proxmire did not accept this argument. "If this is a consideration," he said, "I am appalled, because Lockheed Corporation is
a responsible firm. It is a firm which I think keeps its commitments . . . If it defaults on this contract it seems to me that it
will be plain blackmail. It made a firm commitment to produce
these planes. If the way they get Congress to continue to buy
planes we do not need, and should not have, is to say, 'If you
don't buy these additional planes we're going to default,' then it
seems to me we should have the courage to stand up on our hind
legs and say we will not yield to that kind of blackmail, because
that is exactly what it is."

Referring to the contract as "one of the greatest fiscal disasters
in the history of military contracting," Proxmire tried to impress
upon his colleagues the meaning of the projected $2 billion over-
run. That sum, he said, was three times as much as the federal
government spends on its courts and law enforcement in the entire
country; twice as much as it spends on low and moderate income
housing; nearly as much as all federal expenditures for elementary

and secondary education. "All I'm saying in my amendment," he concluded, "is that before we go ahead with purchasing this squadron we should at least have a study by the GAO to find out what they say as to the cost-effectiveness . . . For the first time in my memory, Congress can do something about an overrun before it is too late. If we fail to act, we have only ourselves to blame."

The following day, California's Senator Murphy reopened the discussion by describing the criticism of the plane as some kind of conspiracy against Lockheed, which has its corporate headquarters in Burbank, California. "In my lifetime," said the former Hollywood song-and-dance man, "I have had the opportunity to become more familiar than most people with publicity or promotive campaigns." Calling many of those campaigns "shoddy," Murphy claimed the critics of the C–5A had mounted "a typical publicity campaign . . . that would rival anything that the Hollywood press agents put on in the old days." He complained that "the innuendoes and images created on those front pages of Washington newspapers linger on, continuing to do damage and disservice to the past fine reputation of Lockheed." He went on to praise Lockheed's integrity at some length, denying several charges that no one had yet made against the company. When he came to the matter of the cost overrun, Senator Murphy vehemently denied the figure of $2 billion, but in a moment of disarming candor, he admitted the whole thing involved "some new type of bookkeeping which I do not understand, and which I would rather not understand, because I do not think it serves good purpose." There was a good deal of such patriotic ignorance throughout the C–5A debate those days. Even the proponents who agreed that the program's cost had grown enormously felt that since the Pentagon said it needed the planes, Congress should authorize funds for them without analyzing that need.

Proxmire, however, continued to attack this point. Citing the

Whittaker Report's assertion that the need for the C–5A is based on the total airlift requirement for the period of 1970 to 1985, he complained that the details upon which the Pentagon arrived at its total force levels are classified. "If we are to act intelligently," he told his fellow senators, "we should know the answers to these questions." One particular passage from the Whittaker Report bothered Proxmire:

> The actual number of aircraft required to achieve rapid deployment objectives is dependent on the number of Army divisions, tactical air units, and support elements to be deployed; the destination of the deployment; the time allowed for deployment; and the other modes of mobility available within the required time.

"How many Army divisions are we talking about?" asked Proxmire. "To know whether we are going to need additional squadrons we should know that. How many tactical air units and support elements are to be deployed? What is the destination of these units? Where are we preparing to send or land such units? What are the consequences of doing that? Are they to be used in another Vietnam? We have been told by the President there are to be no more Vietnams. And in any case, we did not need planes in Vietnam whose only justification was that they could move certain types of materials in ten days or less."

Reminding the Senate that the U.S. already has its heavy armored equipment and other supplies prepositioned in such places as Europe and Korea, he asked, "Is it possible that this plane will get us into far more trouble than it will prevent? Will it involve us in new Vietnams before we have time to consider whether such action is truly in our national interest? Will fast military deployment usurp the prerogatives of the President and Congress, and, on the grounds that since we have a certain capability we should use it, involve us in strife, civil wars, border contretemps and antagonisms where on second thought we would be better advised not to act? The Air Force calls these planes a major instrument of national policy. This Senator asks, 'What national policy?' These questions are at the heart of the matter. Congress should debate them. The military should defend them. The public should challenge them. The country must resolve them before we authorize more planes. My amendment would give us that information."

As fast as Senator Proxmire and his allies could raise such questions about the C–5A's cost, performance, or necessity, the Pentagon hastened to supply answers for the SASC members arguing in support of the program. A memorandum by an Air Force colonel describing these efforts somehow found its way into the *Washington Post*. The memo described a "task force" headed by William Baroody, a special assistant to Secretary Laird, set up "to provide material to Chairman Stennis to refute statements and arguments being made by various Senators in their efforts to reduce or eliminate DoD programs." The memo specifically called for "a point-by-point analysis of the statements made by Senator Proxmire in support of his amendment to eliminate money in 1970 for the fourth squadron of C–5A aircraft." [5]

Much of this material was supplied on a day-to-day basis to meet new points raised during the debate on the C–5A. As fast as Baroody's task force could prepare material for the Pentagon's allies in the Senate, Pentagon couriers rushed it over to the Air Force Office of Legislative Liaison on Capitol Hill. Staff aides from this office then passed the information on to Senator Stennis, or directly to friendly senators in the cloakrooms off the Senate floor. When delivered on the floor, there is rarely any indication of the source of such material. It is generally presented and accepted — at least by the public, if not other congressmen — as the work of the senator or representative who reads it.

The trouble with this system of cooperation between the Penta-

gon and its congressional allies is that what the public sees as a
fair, democratic debate between senators and representatives of
sincerely varying persuasions on military matters is actually a
grossly unequal struggle. Senator Fulbright commented on this
during the debate on the C—5A: "On the one side, questioning the
need for a fourth squadron of the incredibly overpriced C—5A,
as well as other costly new weapons and support systems, are a
group of Senators, aided by a handful of resourceful and dedicated
staff assistants. On the other side is a coalition of conscientious
Senators, supported by the enormous resources of a military
establishment which remains in a state of instant alert for combat
duty on Capitol Hill. In no way do I criticize Senators for accepting information and advice . . . I do, however, feel a good deal
of indignation over the amount of public money and manpower
expended by the Pentagon on political promotion and public relations . . . Since the Pentagon's money is the public's money,
and since Congressmen are the public's representatives, we the
people are essentially paying the Pentagon to convince us to spend
more money on items of excessive cost and dubious necessity."

Despite its generally effective work, the Pentagon's efforts
occasionally backfired. For example, when Senator Goldwater
brought up the comparative cost per ton-mile of the C—5A versus
other forms of cargo transport, he put the figure for the C—5A at
2.9 cents, a remarkably low cost for air freight, compared with
5.3 cents per ton-mile for the smaller C—141. Somewhere along
the line someone must have slipped up, however, for only the day
before Senator Murphy said its cost per ton-mile would be 12
cents. The difference apparently resulted from the fact that
Goldwater's figure did not include the price of the plane itself,
a significant omission. Even the 12-cent figure was misleading,
for it did not include the costs for research and development
on the plane, or the billion dollars' worth of spare parts and

other support items. When these legitimate expenses are included, the C–5A's cost per ton-mile for four squadrons becomes nearly 15 cents. Compared to the cost of shipping military cargo by sea, which runs less than one cent per ton-mile, the C–5A thus becomes an extremely luxurious means of transporting anything but emergency cargo. Subsequent cost increases on the C–5A program have raised the cost per ton-mile to about 20 cents.

As Proxmire, Goldwater, and others debated these points, there were often very few senators around to hear them. Most appeared only for roll calls, and the few in attendance often paid little attention to the debate. Some read it later in the *Congressional Record,* but most didn't bother. They had received the SASC report on the C–5A, and most senators usually go along with the committee. In this case their minds were made up, and they did not want to be confused by cost details or other facts. For example, Ted Stevens, a first-term Republican senator from Alaska, could not understand why there was such a controversy when "the evidence I have seen from the Armed Services Committee seems to indicate that the airplane is being procured at a fair price."

Senator Stevens, as he frequently reminded everyone during his speech, is a former Air Force pilot, and some of his colleagues were thus impressed by his views. "Coming from him," said Senator Goldwater, another Air Force pilot, "these words come from the mouth of an expert, a man who has had practical experience with what we are talking about." Now most of Senator Stevens' practical experience occurred some 25 years ago, when he flew C–47s over China, but Goldwater felt his opinion still carried far more weight than any arguments about the plane's cost. He implied that Senator Proxmire (who served with Army Intelligence during World War II) did not know enough about planes to criticize them. "We have had a great deal of theory expressed on the floor of the Senate," said Goldwater, "from people who really do not know what they are talking about."

The Arizona senator said that despite all the charges about a $2 billion overrun, "no one can be sure" at this time how much the total cost will be. Nevertheless, he concluded: "In my humble opinion — and this statement comes from a conservative — it is very worth while in its cost." How he could conclude this without knowing its cost must be one of the reasons why Mr. Goldwater is considered such an expert on military matters by his colleagues.

The following week, on Tuesday, September 9, the Senate took up the C–5A amendment for the last time. Three hours had been allotted to each side of the debate, and each side had a bit more than one hour left to parcel out among its allies. Senator Symington, one of the C–5A's advocates, led off with a lengthy exposition of the concept of "remote presence" as a guideline for the country's defense policy. He urged a reduction in the number of U.S. military bases abroad, to be replaced by a "massive air-lift" capability that could quickly fly U.S. forces to wherever they were needed. The C–5A, said Symington, would be the key to this new policy. Coming from a former Secretary of the Air Force, this became one of the most powerful arguments against the Proxmire amendment, for nearly every senator — including Proxmire himself — favored a reduction in U.S. forces stationed abroad. Aside from its strategic wisdom, such a policy would help cut the country's balance of payments deficit by reducing the U.S. dollars spent overseas.

Symington's concept of "rapid deployment" also had a powerful appeal for many senators who feel America has a moral obligation to intervene in the affairs of countries around the world under the guise of "keeping the peace." As Senator Herman Talmadge (Dem.-Ga.) said, "If we can have an air capacity with the mobility to transport thousands of troops to any part of the world within a matter of hours, together with their equipment, it will give us a military presence which will be just as adequate as having those troops stationed there all the time."

Senator Fulbright, chairman of the Foreign Relations Committee, strongly opposed this theory of rapid deployment and the C–5A's potential role in it. "The C–5A," said Fulbright, "does not in itself represent a commitment to anybody. But it represents a significant new facility for the making of commitments in the hands of the Executive." Recalling the argument used by Senator Richard Russell to block funds for the Navy's Fast Deployment Logistics ships a few years before, Fulbright warned, "If they can intervene, they will. . . . You are not committing a teenager to an auto wreck by putting him behind the wheel of a hotrod, but you are certainly helping to create a possibility. Before voting over half a billion dollars toward the purchase of a fourth squadron of these spectacularly expensive transport aircraft, Congress has the right and duty to demand full information on their prospective uses. Where, how, and on whose authority does the Administration propose to use these aircraft? Are there in existence contingency plans for their prospective use? . . . Might the Congress be permitted a glimpse of these plans before committing over half a billion dollars to the means of their execution?"

Whatever its strategic merits, the theory of "rapid deployment" has one major fallacy insofar as it calls for the use of C–5As to "bring the boys home." The C–5A is not designed to bring the boys anywhere at all — it is a cargo transport, not a troop transport. The previous week, when SASC member Peter Dominick had spoken of using the C–5A to "get some of our troops out of Western Europe," Senator Goldwater had quickly reminded him that "the C–5A is not a troop transport. It would move equipment, not troops." This time Goldwater was silent, and the

Symington argument proved to be persuasive. Even the eminent
senator from Georgia, Richard Russell declared, "I want to say
here and now, that people who really mean it when they say we
should bring these troops home had better provide for the airlift,
because you are not going to be able to bring them home until
you have some means to send them back." Minority leader Hugh
Scott, who also should have known better, told the Senate's opponents of the Vietnam war, "If you want to bring the boys home,
there must be vehicles to bring them home in, and the C—5A is
the largest available vehicle." Somehow Senator Scott seemed
unable to imagine these troops coming home by the same planes
and ships that had managed to bring them over in the first place.
No one in the Pentagon or the White House had ever suggested
their departure or the war's end was being delayed for lack of
suitable transport. Besides, the C—5A would not be available for
another two or three years anyway, by which time most senators
hoped to see the Vietnam war ended.

The most vulnerable part of the Proxmire amendment was its
request for the General Accounting Office to determine the
military necessity for the fourth squadron of C—5As. As Senator
Cannon said, "I doubt very much that the GAO has the competence to make the military judgment which the Proxmire
amendment requires." Senator Fulbright facetiously asked SASC
chairman Stennis if he felt "anyone outside of the military establishment itself is competent" to make such a judgment. He
implied that Congress would be abdicating its duty to examine
military legislation if it agreed that only the Pentagon has sufficient wisdom to pass judgment on military matters.

Senator John Pastore (Dem.-R.I.) claimed Proxmire was trying
"to make the GAO assume the function of the Joint Chiefs of
Staff, and become the military deciding agency of this great
nation of ours." Though Senator Pastore was obviously unwilling

to rely on the wisdom of the GAO, he was only too eager to accept the authority of the Senate Armed Services Committee. He asked Margaret Chase Smith, the SASC's ranking GOP member, if she was convinced of the C–5A's quality and the Pentagon's need for it. Mrs. Smith, obviously pleased at this genuflection to her authority, replied, "Yes, absolutely." She then admitted, "Of course I can only take the word of those who know much more about it than I do," which meant the Air Force. Pastore later told reporters, "I wanted the best military advice on the matter. That's why you heard me ask Mrs. Smith." [6]

Near the end of the debate on the C–5A, Senator Stennis claimed that delaying the purchase of the fourth squadron would set the entire program back more than a year and would actually raise the cost even further. The Air Force provided Stennis with an estimate of $400 to $500 million as the additional expense that such a delay would cause. However, considering the accuracy of their previous cost estimates on the C–5A, one must wonder why anyone would accept this one. Proxmire argued that since the first 58 planes would not even be completed for another two to three years, a brief delay at this point could hardly cause that much trouble. In fact it seems odd that the Air Force could be so concerned about a three-month delay for a GAO investigation, when it had not expressed any alarm over what would probably be a one-year "slippage" in Lockheed's delivery schedule.

Despite all the arguments by Proxmire and the C–5A's other critics, the general feeling among most senators was that the plane itself was excellent, and that regardless of how much the costs had risen, it was too late now to back out. Even Senator Symington conceded the planes might be "a poor buy," but insisted they were "important to our national security." Senator Smith concluded that "if we are to make the best of a bad situation, it is better to recoup as much as possible from the C–5 investment rather than to kill the program." Proxmire tried to explain that his amendment would not "kill" the program, or even delay production on the 58 planes already authorized, but no one seemed to hear him.

In his concluding speech, Proxmire tried to convince the Senate that his only purpose was to get the answers to some significant questions concerning the C–5A before authorizing the additional funds. "It is clear," he said, "that Congress cannot at the present time make an intelligent judgment about the facts in this case. The Air Force has systematically hidden the facts about the C–5A." He pointed out that the Air Force had concealed the cost overrun for several years, had lied to Congress about it the year before, and was still using cost estimates more than a year old. "In light of the shocking record of bad faith on the part of the Air Force, it simply cannot be relied upon by the Congress for the true facts about this program . . . The Air Force has deceived and misled the Congress in this matter again and again . . . Now is the time to obtain the facts about the C–5A from a new source, independent of the Air Force . . . A monumental record of inept management, waste and inefficiency has already been established in this program. After the billions of taxpayers' dollars that have been expended on the C–5A, the public is entitled to some assurance that future expenditures are absolutely essential to national security . . . At present, no member of the Senate can assure his constituency of the need for pouring yet more billions of dollars into the C–5A program. No Senator can in good faith tell the people of his state what the C–5A will cost. No Senator can truthfully say that the fourth squadron of C–5As is economically or militarily justified."

By the end of Proxmire's speech, late in the afternoon, everyone seemed to be exhausted with the question of the C–5A, and both sides agreed to terminate the debate. On a roll-call vote, the

Senate overwhelmingly rejected the Proxmire amendment by a vote of 64 to 23. Since most observers had expected a much closer vote, recalling the one-vote margin on the ABM, there was considerable surprise at the margin of defeat on the C–5A amendment. Senator Pastore, however, later asked reporters, "Why are you surprised that there were so few votes? It's just that little clique against Vietnam." [7]

CHAPTER TEN
Rivers Delivers the House

"Shame on this House!"

Representative Andrew Jacobs

COMPARED TO the Senate debate on the 1970 military procurement bill, the House debate was a farce. *The Nation* described it in an editorial as "a new abyss in representative government." [1] The Senate spent more than two months on the bill, with four days devoted to consideration of the Proxmire amendment on the C–5A. The House took three days to dispose of the entire $21.3 billion authorization, which loyal HASC members considered ample time. They saw no reason why the decisions they had reached in their infinite wisdom should be tampered with or even questioned by the other 400 members of the House. The relatively free debate just concluded in the Senate struck them as a waste of time. [2]

As in every other military matter that comes before the House, one man had absolute control over the debate — Mendel Rivers. He ran it with about as much grace as a South Carolina tobacco auctioneer. There was never any question of votes, for he knew he had far more than he needed. Therefore he saw no reason to waste time on the civilities of discussion. He simply rammed the bill through, as he had always done in the past. Though the HASC hearings had ended nearly two months before, the committee did not release its report on the bill until two days before debate opened in the House. Few Congressmen had time to study the 145-page report carefully, and even fewer bothered to read the 4361-page record of the actual hearings. Expecting this, the five liberal critics on the committee filed their own 29-page minority report, attacking certain items in the bill.

Rivers told the House Rules Committee, which determines the amount of time allotted for debate, that three hours would be plenty for consideration of the $23.1 billion measure. Due to the press of other business, and because they were not informed in time of the Rules Committee hearings, no one from the opposition (or, as Rivers referred to them, "the bleeding heart society") showed up to argue for more time. When Representative Thomas O'Neill (Dem.-Mass.), a member of the Rules Committee, suggested that ten hours would allow for a more rational discussion, Rivers insisted that no additional time was necessary. The Rules Committee finally "compromised" on four hours for general debate, with *five minutes* for each amendment. According to custom, the time would be "equally divided and controlled by the chairman and ranking minority member" of the HASC. Since its ranking GOP member is Illinois Representative Leslie Arends, a man whose views on military affairs rarely differ from those of chairman Rivers, this left Rivers in virtual control of the entire debate, an arrangement he found perfectly satisfactory.

Representative O'Neill and many other congressmen did not. When the bill first came up on Wednesday, October 1, for the vote on the Rules Committee's decision, O'Neill objected to "the great mistake I believe we are making here today. We are going to discuss an authorization of more than $21 billion for military procurement and for new weapons that may mean an entirely new defense and military policy. Four hours is simply not enough . . . we would be spending at a rate of almost five and a half billion dollars an hour . . . It is the largest procurement bill that has ever come before the Congress or before any legislative body in the annals of history. There is disagreement among the Members as to the worth of these systems and equipment . . . Yesterday our committee was told that there is no need for additional time, that each member of this body knows how he is going to vote on the bill. This may be true, but I doubt it. . . . I do not believe that intelligent debate will have no effect on Members' decisions."

Representative John Moss (Dem.-Calif.) complained that except for the members of the HASC, the rest of the members of the House "do not have the chance of the proverbial snowball in hell of addressing themselves to the issues contained in this legislation . . . I think it is time that this House become concerned over the role it is being relegated to: that of less and less significance in the government of the United States; that of less and less significance in the legislative process of the United States. We are being forced time and time again to consider under conditions of limitation the most far-reaching policy commitments any legislative body in the world is called upon to consider . . . Must it always be said of the House that it fails to consider; that it does not know what it is doing; that it does not act upon the facts? The other body, with unrestricted debate, has the opportunity for every Member to gain the knowledge he should have as an effective legislator. I say to every Member of this body that there is no issue upon which you are receiving a greater volume of mail today than those which are contained in this bill. We ought to know what we are doing. We ought to have adequate time to engage in a meaningful debate, and not be forced to compact it all into four hours . . . If we debated this thing for a week we would be giving it inadequate attention."

The prospect of debating the military procurement bill for one week obviously did not please most members of the House. The Majority Leader, Representative Carl Albert (Dem.-Okla.), dropped a gentle hint that if the House did not complete debate on the bill by the following day, it would have to remain in session on Friday, cutting short the House's normal three-day weekend. Albert assured everyone he did not wish to "cut anyone off," but he just felt that he should "make this announcement at this time so Members may be advised accordingly." They were, approving the ruling on a four-hour debate by a vote of 324 to 61.

Mendel Rivers helped achieve this vote by assuring everyone that his committee had examined every detail of the bill with great care and that the rest of the House could safely rely on its wisdom. He claimed that the liberals on the committee had had ample opportunity to present their views. "Everyone had his time," said Rivers. "As a matter of fact, some people probably had more time than they deserved." Calling these liberal critics "Johnny-come-lately military experts," he warned the House: "This is your military. If you do not want to provide for it, then go ahead. This is your military and this is your Committee on the Armed Services. If you want to repudiate us, that is your responsibility."

Rivers opened the general debate that afternoon with an attack on those who would cut military spending in such "critical" times. He generously assured everyone that he favored a certain amount of public questioning on military matters, but he felt such questioning had become "dangerously excessive." He called it "antimilitarism gone berserk. Experts are mushrooming all over the place like toadstools. I have run across more experts in the last year than there are dogs at a county fair." He warned the House, "We are not in a debating society now. The question now is preparation for survival."

Referring to the C–5A, Rivers did not bother with facts. He

merely proclaimed: "I want the C–5A . . . This is the largest plane ever built, and it will work just as sure as you are a foot high." Representative Tom Steed, an Oklahoma Democrat whose district includes Altus Air Force Base, where the C–5As would undergo flight testing (and where the local high school had just been renamed "Mendel Rivers High"), announced his whole-hearted support for the program. He claimed the C–5A was desperately needed to replace many air transports which he described as "grossly inefficient and hopelessly obsolete." (Even the Pentagon might dispute this remark.) In addition to this strategic argument, Steed offered another, much closer to home: "All of the people of the Fourth Congressional District of Oklahoma are looking forward to welcoming the C–5A at Altus Air Force Base." Mr. Steed obviously considered their eagerness for the C–5A as compelling an argument in its favor as the Air Force's allegedly desperate need for it.

The next speaker to advocate passage of the C–5A authorization was HASC member, Representative Donald Clancy (Rep.-Ohio). He claimed the plane would meet all its performance requirements and that its cost overrun was largely due to "mitigating circumstances over which neither the Air Force nor the contractor had any control." Mr. Clancy did not inform the House that his Cincinnati district includes General Electric's Evendale plant, where the C–5A engines are being produced. "I believe," said Clancy, "that the C–5A will put this country years ahead in airlift technology. It is more than the world's largest airplane. It's a new kind of defense system . . . It's like having a military base in nearly every strategic spot on the globe." If this language sounds familiar to some readers it should, for it is identical — word for word — to a Lockheed advertisement for the C–5A quoted earlier in this book.

When Otis Pike rose to speak during this general debate time, he admitted he was "one of those who may be classified as a bleeding heart, or a Johnny-come-lately, or a non-expert, or something like that." Describing the $21.3 billion defense authorization as "too much money for us to be spending in this area at this time," he pointed out that for the cost of just one C–5A, his Long Island district could build four schools for 1000 pupils each and operate them for 30 years.

General debate on the entire bill ended that afternoon. On Thursday morning, at ten o'clock, the House reconvened to consider the amendments, which Rivers said were "not worth dignifying with debate." On the amendment to halt deployment of the ABM, limiting funds to research and development, each member had five minutes to state his case. Rivers allowed this time grudgingly, claiming that "everyone has made up his mind on how he is going to vote on just about everything here." This was probably true, and even the sponsors of the cost-cutting amendments knew it.

After a few hours of five-minute speeches, the House voted down the anti-ABM amendment by a solid 219 to 105. Since this same measure had been defeated in the Senate by only one vote, after considerable pressure from the Nixon administration, the margin of its rejection by the House gave a clear indication of the fate of the other amendments. By a vote of 131 to 92, the House also rejected an attempt by Defense critics to delete a billion dollars for ship construction that Rivers had added to the bill against the advice of the Pentagon. An equally crushing fate befell an attempt to block funds for the Cobra, a controversial Army attack helicopter. In his typical defense of this program, Rivers claimed, "We need those Cobras more than we need breath itself. If we do not need this helicopter, we do not need any rifles in South Vietnam. My goodness! What are we talking about? If you take this away from the U.S. Army, you might as well tell them to come home."

When Representative Robert Leggett moved to cut development

funds for a new manned strategic bomber (AMSA), Rivers raised
the specter of a Russian bomber attack, insisting that if they have
them we must have them. Leggett pointed out that the Pentagon
itself had recently reported the Russians were no longer building
such bombers. Angered by this public questioning of his judgment, Rivers fumed, "I will not discuss the AMSA. I will not
discuss with you what the Russians have. On my own responsibility I tell you the Russians are building a bomber. You can take
it or leave it." Most of the House took it and approved the funds
for AMSA.

As the afternoon wore on, Rivers, with the active cooperation
of House Speaker John McCormack (Dem.-Mass.) and Minority
Leader Gerald Ford (Rep.-Mich.), began cutting off debate on
the amendments, forcing many members to state their views in a
matter of minutes or even seconds. When Representative Henry
Reuss (Dem.-Wisc.) tried to explain his proposal to cut funds for
an airborne radar system, the House Speaker gavelled him down
after only 45 seconds. Even Reuss' Republican opponents were
appalled at this treatment. Illinois Representative John Anderson, leader of the House GOP Conference, jumped to his feet
and yelled, "This is an outrage!" This is nothing but a gag rule."
Representative Andrew Jacobs (Dem.-Ind.) shouted, "Shame!
Shame on this House! A civilized society does not stifle opposition. It meets it."

By the time Otis Pike rose to offer his C–5A amendment,
similar to that which Proxmire had introduced in the Senate,
cutting out funds for the fourth squadron, Rivers tried to close off
the discussion quickly. While several of Pike's allies objected,
Pike himself had no doubts about the outcome: "I am not at all
sure that prolonging this debate at this time is particularly useful,
because we can see the way things are going. By the same token
I think there are things which ought to be said, and which are

important not only to us who have worked hard on these matters
. . . but that are important to the nation as a whole.

"You have all heard about the C–5A aircraft. I am not going
to change any votes by a speech I make here today. It has
fantastic capabilities. It has fantastic cost overruns . . . The
question again is one of national priorities. How much is it worth
to us?" Explaining that current estimates for the plane came to
about $45 million each, Pike simply asked, "Is it worth what we
are paying for it?" Quoting from Lockheed ads that a fleet of
C–5As could move an army across an ocean in hours, he said,
"If I read my mail right, the only direction that my people want
to move an army across an ocean is toward home. I do not think
they really care if it is in a matter of hours. I think they would
be willing to spend even a few days on it."

For those who had followed the Senate debate on the C–5A,
there was not much new said either in support of or against the
program. Advocates praised the plane's alleged performance and
stressed the military's need for it. Opponents questioned this
need and stressed the cost overruns. Addressing himself to the
need for a fourth squadron of C–5As, Representative John Moss
(Dem.-Cal.) pointed out that the Pentagon could purchase two
747s for the cost of each C–5A. He also reminded his colleagues
that in an emergency the Defense Department can always call on
the country's civilian cargo fleet, which generally operates at less
than 50 per cent capacity.

The only new points made were generally either untrue or
irrelevant. Representative William Randall (Dem.-Mo.) in-
correctly accused Pike of trying to cut out the C–5A program
entirely. Representative Phil Landrum (Dem.-Ga.) praised
Lockheed's board chairman Daniel Haughton as "a former Alabama boy, and a very distinguished man of business, who
worked his way through college." Representative John Davis

(Dem.-Ga.), whose district includes the Lockheed-Georgia plant at Marietta, claimed that press accounts of the C-5A cost overrun and other problems had been mainly "distortions, half-truths, and gross inaccuracies."

About five o'clock in the afternoon, Rivers rose to demand that debate on the C-5A be limited to 15 more minutes. This meant that each remaining member who wished to speak had the luxury of condensing his argument into a pithy 75 seconds. Rivers considered this perfectly adequate, for he could see no reason why anyone would attack the C-5A. "This plane is no failure," he insisted. "There is nothing to compare with it since man took to the air down at Kitty Hawk, North Carolina. . . . This is no pipe dream. It is a fact of life. Our committee has gone into this thing . . . There is nothing in the world like it. We are not selling you a bag of bones." As for the $2 billion overrun, Rivers considered it unimportant. "As everyone knows, there are overruns on everything. Overruns are no mortal sin . . . We have got to have this thing, whether or not there are overruns."

Representative William Moorhead, who had spent nearly a year studying the C-5A, now had all of 75 seconds in which to present to his colleagues the fruits of his labor. All he really had time for was to request permission from the chair to extend his remarks later in *The Congressional Record*. While this made interesting reading for those willing to read it days later, it could have no effect on the House vote on the amendment to cut off funds for additional C-5As. To the surprise of no one, the House rejected the Pike amendment 136 to 60.

By similarly comfortable margins the legislators voted down every other attempt to reduce the Pentagon's shopping list. Opponents were unable to cut a single penny out of the $21.3 billion package prepared by the House Armed Services Committee. A number of amendments that had been passed overwhelmingly by the Senate were rejected by the House, including one that merely called for a study of profits in the defense industry. Saddened by this display, Representative Andrew Jacobs could only say, "My, my, my. How badly some do not want to talk about studying the profits of defense contractors."

As a result of their complete impotence in the face of the monolithic House leadership, and under the pressure of trying to state their views in a few seconds, many of the defense critics grew bitter. As the afternoon wore on, tempers began to flare and opponents exchanged harsh words which they later deleted from *The Congressional Record*.[3] Mendel Rivers made a particularly vicious attack on Robert Leggett, the California Democrat who as one of the HASC's "fearless five" had emerged from the debate as one of the leaders of the opposition to the C–5A and other items in the arms budget. Unaccustomed to what he considered disloyalty and ingratitude from one of his own committee members, Rivers openly threatened Leggett on the House floor. He reminded the California Democrat of how many jobs the Defense Department controlled at the five military bases in Leggett's district and warned him that the military has "a capacity for knowing who their friends are." Congressmen present at that moment were shocked at such a naked display of the kind of politics normally conducted with some discretion. Representative John Moss told Rivers that the entire 21-man California Democratic delegation in the House would back Leggett. "Let there be any retaliation against that delegation, and by God we'll fight you all the way!" Moss shouted. Faced with this threat of united opposition, Rivers apologized to Leggett, withdrew his own threat, and deleted his attack from the *Record*.

Many members of the House were disgusted and ashamed by the manner in which Rivers and the House leadership bludgeoned the minority who opposed them on the military procurement bill.

One congressman later observed privately that if the American people had been watching the debate that day, most members of the House would be seeking new employment next year. One of the members most appalled was freshman representative Allard Lowenstein (Dem.-N.Y.): "I speak with some sadness as this comes to a conclusion," he said at the close of the debate. "I love this place. To be elected to it is easily the greatest honor I shall expect to attain. Yet much that happens here leaves me feeling that we are not conducting ourselves as we should . . . We have greater obligations to the country than has been shown by our behavior today." [4]

CHAPTER ELEVEN

The Pentagon Retreats

"The Defense Department announced today a substantial reduction in its controversial C–5A supertransport program, which had encountered widespread criticism because of its soaring costs . . . An Air Force spokesman declined to estimate the saving gained from the cutback."

The New York Times,
November 15, 1969

IF THE LAST FEW CHAPTERS have left the impression that the Defense Department can get anything it wants out of Congress, one should not presume the Pentagon is unaware of or unconcerned about opposition. The friendly relations between the Pentagon and Congress depend in part upon Defense officials' having sufficient wisdom to avoid requests that create politically embarrassing controversy. For controversy creates public opposition, which to most congressmen is even worse than congressional opposition. While most congressmen are generally only too willing to go along with military requests to "insure national security," they must also worry about their own security with voters back home. In a time of increasing public concern over military spending, the C–5A had become a political liability. Thus, while the Pentagon's procurement strategists were pleased with the C–5A's successful flight through the Armed Services Committees' hearings and the floor debates, they did worry about the considerable flak it drew from critics in Congress and the press. They began to talk about a strategic withdrawal, in the form of a cutoff at four squadrons, or 81 planes, instead of the six squadrons, or 115 planes, originally planned.

Rumors about such a decision were already circulating during the congressional debate on the C–5A that fall. When questioned about them, Pentagon spokesmen told the press the Defense Department had "not yet decided" whether to buy the fifth and sixth squadrons. Just before the House began its October, 1969, debate on the military procurement bill, Deputy Secretary of Defense David Packard told HASC chairman Rivers that DoD would not need the $52 million included for long lead-time items for the fifth squadron, and the money was removed from the House version of the bill. However, by the time the final bill emerged from the joint Senate-House conference a few weeks later, the $52 million had somehow gotten back in.[1]

Finally, on Friday, November 14, 1969, the Defense Department formally announced its decision to limit the program to four squadrons, or 81 planes. Those who wondered what had prompted the decision found a reason the following Monday, when Ernest Fitzgerald testified again at a new round of hearings by the Proxmire subcommittee. Fitzgerald claimed that the latest Air Force estimate for the cost of the entire 115-plane program had grown to $5.8 billion — an increase of $600 million since the previous official estimates.[2] If Fitzgerald knew about this new estimate, the Pentagon certainly did also. Probably foreseeing a renewal of the controversy over the C–5A, DoD officials undoubtedly felt the time had come to cut back the program.

While the Pentagon's Public Affairs Office and the press treated the decision as a "cutback" or "reduction" in the C–5A program, estimating it would "save" more than a billion dollars, the reduction and savings were purely imaginary. According to Air Force testimony, no one had actually ordered the planes yet, or even asked for the money. Besides, even the "reduced" buy of 81 planes would still cost at least half a billion dollars more than the original cost estimate for the entire 115 planes. (The Pentagon often achieves impressive savings in this fashion, simply by not doing something it has previously only talked about doing.)

Senator Proxmire greeted the news of the C–5A "cutback" with obvious satisfaction: "I'm delighted the Air Force has decided to stop the C–5A program at 81 planes, a course of action I proposed, but the Pentagon fought, during the Senate debate on the C–5A." [3] Proxmire had good reason to be satisfied. Most observers and officials close to the C–5A program agree that without the publicity resulting from his subcommittee hearings, the Pentagon would have never even considered stopping short of the full 115-plane order.

Lockheed, of course, felt little satisfaction at the Pentagon's decision. According to Air Force figures (which Lockheed disputed) the company would lose about $500 million if the C–5A program stopped at 81 planes. As its officials had testified before the Armed Services Committees, Lockheed felt that in exercising its option for Run B, the Air Force had in effect already ordered the full 115 planes, subject only to congressional authorization of funds. Since Congress had not yet blocked or even considered the funding for the fourth and fifth squadrons, the decision to stop at 81 planes was entirely the Pentagon's. In the view of Lockheed's lawyers, the Air Force had thus illegally defaulted on its C–5A contract. Lockheed protested the decision by filing an appeal notice with the Armed Services Board of Contract Appeals, advising its stockholders that the "completion of the C–5A program, with no major financial loss, depends on the legal interpretation of the contract." Lockheed-Georgia president Thomas May announced, "We are confident our interpretation will be upheld." [4]

Not all Lockheed officials shared Mr. May's confidence. Early in December, 1969, Lockheed board chairman Daniel Haughton met with Defense Secretary Laird to "explain" the company's problems. A few weeks later, a delegation of political and business leaders from Georgia's Cobb County flew up to Washington for a session at the Pentagon with Deputy Secretary Packard. Their concern resulted largely from the fact that as the C–5A had moved from development into production, Lockheed-Georgia had already laid off 5000 men. The cutback brought an immediate loss of another 1100 jobs, with more layoffs likely.[5]

Packard told the Georgia delegation the decision to cut back the C–5A program to 81 planes was final, but he did offer some consolation. In order to ease the effect of the cutback on Lockheed, Marietta, and Cobb County, the Defense Department would "entertain" a proposal suggested by Haughton earlier — to slow down or "stretch out" production by allowing Lockheed-Georgia to produce two planes a month instead of three.[6] (The program had already been slowed from the four planes a month required by the contract to three because of Lockheed's technical problems.) The new stretch-out would cost the Air Force an additional $75 million[7] and would mean at least another year's delay in the delivery of what Mendel Rivers had once described as a "crash program." Obviously, the C–5A's importance to the financial security of Georgia outweighed the military's supposedly urgent need for it.

The C–5A production stretch-out to January, 1973, was just as vital to Lockheed as it was to Georgia. Lockheed had clearly bought in low on the C–5A in the hope of making up any losses on the military contract by producing a lucrative commercial version. But the company needed time to build up orders for at least 50 of these commercial L–500s before committing itself to their production. These orders had not yet come in. If the Pentagon had stuck to the delivery schedule of the original C–5A contract, the cutback to 81 planes would have meant huge layoffs and a costly shutdown of the Marietta plant before enough orders came in to start production on the L–500. The C–5A production stretch-out would allow for more gradual layoffs, and would give the company an extra year to gather orders for the L–500.

President May said his salesmen expected to sell as many as 300 L–500s at a price of $23.5 million each (a remarkable bargain considering that Lockheed was changing the Air Force at least double that price for essentially the same plane). If true, the L–500s would bring in roughly $7 billion, with much of the company's initial research and development cost already paid for by the Air Force — or rather, the American taxpayers. The potential profit on such a venture would easily cover the loss of a paltry few million dollars on the C–5A contract.

At an Atlanta press conference in February, 1970, Lockheed announced the promotion of Mr. May from president of Lockheed-Georgia to "senior vice-president for administration" of Lockheed Aircraft, the California-based parent company. Since he retired soon afterward, one might wonder whether this move did in fact represent a promotion, or the desire for new management for the embattled C–5A program. As the company's "father of the C–5A," May was identified with all the plane's troubles, and Lockheed might well have felt a corporate face lifting would improve the program's image. As though he realized this possibility, May used the occasion of his farewell remarks to defend the C–5A program and to blast its critics. He insisted the plane would save "billions of dollars" and would help the United States to maintain peace around the world. He said comments by "certain Congressmen" that the plane was unsafe were "far from the fact, and insulting." [9]

If institutional giants like Lockheed can indeed be insulted by criticism, they also have considerable means for soothing their corporate egos. To counter the disastrous publicity resulting from the cost overrun, the cutback, and growing technical problems with the plane itself, Lockheed's public relations department tried hard to repair the image of the C–5A. At aerospace industry meetings, they showed excellent films of the plane performing such aerodynamic feats as takeoff, flight, and landing. Ads in industry trade magazines hailed successive achievements in the test program as marvels of technology, instead of attempts to satisfy the still unfulfilled performance requirements of the contract. During this same period many of the C–5A's subcontractors, including several of those responsible for its defective parts, also took full-page ads in the trade magazine to congratulate themselves on their participation in the program.

Along with this publicity campaign, Lockheed devoted a great deal of time and energy to figuring out ways to sell more C–5As to the Defense Department, despite the cutback. Company spokesmen told some reporters that one reason for the production slowdown was to give the Air Force more time to consider "follow-on orders" for more C–5As. On the face of it, such reasoning seems highly illogical, but since the Air Force often acts in illogical ways, one cannot be sure. The Lockheed PR men may have known something the rest of us didn't. There may well have been an understanding with the Air Force that in a year or so, when the public controversy over the C–5A would hopefully settle down, the Pentagon would decide that it really did need the fifth and sixth squadrons after all.

In case anyone at the Pentagon was wondering what to do with some extra C–5As, Lockheed had plenty of ideas, most of them the fruits of feasibility studies financed by the Defense Department. In other words, at the same time the Pentagon announced a cutback in its orders for C–5As as an economy move, it was also paying Lockheed millions of dollars to dream up additional uses for the plane that would justify increased orders — and sales for Lockheed.

Threatened by the cutback, Lockheed quickly developed a number of what it called "corollary missions" for the C–5A.[10] The company produced scale models of the plane in various ingenious configurations designed to illustrate its potential uses: troop transport, aerial tanker, emergency command post, missile launching platform, nuclear bomber, seaplane, minelayer, airborne radar center, and many other imaginative possibilities. Lockheed officials pushed hard on the aerial tanker idea, suggesting a potential sale of 200 planes for this use alone. They pointed out that a redesigned C–5A could carry 332,000 pounds of fuel — nearly three times as much as the largest current aerial tanker, Boeing's KC–135. As a triple-decked airborne command post it could spend up to three days in the air with in-flight refueling. As a triple-decked troop transport it could carry 600 to 800 men. Modified as a bomber, it could carry more than four times the bomb load of the B–52s now littering the Vietnamese countryside with less than pinpoint precision.

Those who could recall Lockheed's testimony during the congressional hearings found this new sales pitch amusing. Only a few months before, the company had defended the plane's excessive costs on the grounds that its peculiar functions as an air cargo transport required many highly specialized and costly features. Because of its supposedly unique design, no other aircraft could match its capabilities. Suddenly, with the need for finding other functions, the C–5A's design had become much less unique, permitting all sorts of "easy modifications." Lockheed's past record with the C–5A gave little assurance that such modifications would be either easy or cheap, and while they might change its function, they would still not make the plane a bargain.

CHAPTER TWELVE
Cracked Wings and Other
Unforeseen Technical Difficulties

*"The important thing is that the basic design and
structure of the C–5 are sound."*

Robert Fuhrman
President, Lockheed-Georgia Company

BY ORDERING the cutback to 81 planes, Pentagon officials must
have felt they had put an end to most of the criticism of the C–5A.
For thoughout all the congressional hearings and floor debate its
critics had concentrated on either the cost or the number of planes
in the program — both of which would be "reduced" by the cutback. Hardly anyone had attacked the quality of the C–5A itself. Its advocates had used its supposedly superior performance
as a major argument in its defense.

Back in January, 1969, Assistant Secretary of the Air Force
Robert Charles told the Proxmire subcommittee the C–5A would
"exceed the contractor's proposed performance . . . and will
also exceed his contractual commitments . . . I know of no
other aircraft program where the record has been so good." [1] In
April, when they appeared before the House Military Operations
Subcommittee, USAF officials were still bubbling over with en-
thusiasm for the plane's prospective performance. Aaron Racusin,
Deputy Assistant Secretary for Procurement, told the subcommittee, "as far as I know right now, with respect to technical performance, they [Lockheed] are one per cent in excess of their
contractual commitments. And that is better than any other
weapons system we have heretofore obtained."

When Congressman Moorhead pressed this point, however, Racusin backed off a bit:

> Rep. Moorhead: Mr. Secretary, is the C–5 living up to its performance specifications? I mean the sink rate, the kind of terrain it can land on, and so forth.
>
> Mr. Racusin: I believe that I will defer here to General Goldsworthy [Commander of the Air Force's Aeronautical Systems Division] or to Colonel Beckman [director of the C–5 System Program Office] who live with it every day.
>
> General Goldsworthy: The answer is "Yes," and we can give you specifics. Colonel Beckman can give you specifics, but the answer is "Yes."
>
> Rep. Moorhead: It is living up to its original performance specifications?
>
> Col. Beckman: According to our best estimates at this time, sir.[2]

With such buck-passing evasiveness the Air Force managed to fend off these early inquiries about the plane's quality and performance. But by the time of the HASC hearings in May, a few hints began to appear, suggesting the Galaxy might have a few problems in addition to its cost. When General Thomas Jeffrey, Air Force Deputy Chief of Staff, explained a delay in the plane's delivery schedule by citing certain "quality control problems" at Lockheed, Representative Alexander Pirnie (Rep.-N.Y.) could not accept this explanation:

> Rep. Pirnie: Didn't the Air Force have inspectors there currently, as this was progressing?
>
> Gen. Jeffrey: The system that the Air Force . . .
>
> Rep. Pirnie: Can't you answer that question directly? Did you, or did you not have inspectors that were watching the [C–5A's] progress?
>
> Gen. Jeffrey: We did not have inspectors that are watching every detail of the contractor's actions, Mr. Pirnie.
>
> Rep. Pirnie: I didn't ask you that, General. You know what I'm seeking to get the answer to. Don't you have inspectors as the work is progressing?

Gen. Jeffrey: Yes sir, we do.
Rep. Pirnie: Why would it take you by surprise?

General Jeffrey explained that the Air Force inspectors are only responsible for an "overview" of the company's quality control system, rather than for checking the actual work in progress. "So a quality control problem could go for a period undetected."

Rep. Pirnie: So maybe the system ought to be revised?
Gen. Jeffrey: Sir, I think we've got a good system.
Rep. Pirnie: This isn't a good result.[3]

In June, 1969, at the hearings of the SASC, Air Force witnesses still described the planes as an unqualified success, but still passed the buck when questions became too specific. Air Force Secretary Seamans assured the committee "the aircraft itself is proving to be excellent, fully capable of performing its mission." Chairman Stennis, who by then had probably heard rumors about the plane's technical problems, asked if Seamans had consulted any engineering experts outside the Air Force before making such a "sweeping" judgment. "I myself have not done so," replied Seamans. "I am relying on information that has been reported directly to me by the project people in the Air Force." (Since these same project people had been suppressing reports about the plane's cost difficulties, it is surprising that anyone, particularly Seamans, would rely on their assurances as to its technical excellence.)

Stennis asked Seamans, "As Secretary of the Air Force, don't you think it is your duty before you reach a final conclusion on these matters to consult with someone beyond the Air Force itself?" Seamans agreed and told the committee about the Whittaker review, which would be a "searching" look at the entire C-5A program, using outside consultants.[4] Stennis then asked Assistant Secretary Whittaker, "Does this machine give every evidence that it will do the job?" Whittaker, despite having held his own job at that time for only 30 days, assured Stennis that he had complete confidence in the C–5A. On the basis of his own hasty investigation, an actual flight in the plane, and the projections of the joint USAF-Lockheed flight test program, he predicted a performance level of exactly "101 per cent" of the contract requirements[5] — not 100 per cent, but 101 per cent.

Since no concrete evidence of technical or performance troubles had emerged at this time, these undocumented assertions apparently convinced most committee members. As in nearly all congressional studies of weapons procurement, Congress simply had no other source of information than the officials who appeared in defense of the programs. As Senator George Murphy admitted, "I am relying upon the judgment of the experts that this is a good airplane." [6] By "experts" he meant the Air Force officials responsible for the C–5A — the same men whose careers would be jeopardized if Congress began to suspect that in addition to its cost difficulties, the plane was not living up to its performance requirements.

Besides the Air Force, Lockheed also would have been hurt by any disclosure of performance problems on the C–5A. So when the company's officials testified before the armed services committees, they also stressed its technical excellence, and the committees believed them. After Lockheed board chairman Daniel Haughton testified, Senator Strom Thurmond (Rep.-S.C.) told him, "This would be a sad hearing indeed if Lockheed had not developed a fine aircraft . . . We do have something to be thankful for on this contract. You have apparently come up with a very fine aircraft." [7]

Those who attended the hearings of the June, 1969, Proxmire subcommittee a few days later heard Ernest Fitzgerald give the first public evidence that the C–5A might not be the very fine

aircraft that Lockheed and the Air Force claimed. Fitzgerald
spoke of "quite a large number of contract changes" and said he
had heard that "there have been some relaxations of requirements." Asked to document these charges, Fitzgerald checked
with the Air Force and was told of three such changes that affected the plane's performance: a slight increase in its weight, a
15 per cent decrease in the maximum speed for lowering flaps on
landing, and a 10 per cent decrease in the allowable "sink rate"
on landing. Each of these changes represented a clear reduction
in the plane's performance standards.[8]

Unsatisfied with this response, Fitzgerald pressed the Air Force
for more information on contract changes. In July, 1969, after
four weeks of wrangling, and after the Proxmire hearings were
over, he finally received a more complete summary which showed
a total of 46 changes in the plane's design and performance, plus
789 changes in its specifications.[9] When asked recently if this
was unusual, Fitzgerald replied, "The C–5A is no worse than
most other programs, in this respect. When the contractor has
trouble meeting the contract specifications, the Air Force usually
agrees to change them. The contract merely serves to accom-
modate what the contractor does. If there's a conflict, the contract will be changed. What really happens is that instead of the
plane meeting the specifications, the specifications meet the
plane."

A few weeks later, in July, the Air Force released the Whittaker Report on the C–5A, which specifically denied that any
USAF-authorized contract changes had resulted in "a degradation of performance requirements." In apparent support of this
claim, however, the report went on to list ten contract changes
which quite clearly reduced the plane's performance. For example,
one of them called for a 15 per cent reduction in its gross (including cargo) weight for takeoff and landing on substandard airfields.

Since the C–5A's most heralded virtue is its supposed ability to carry huge cargo loads in and out of such primitive airstrips, a 15 per cent reduction in its cargo capacity in such conditions definitely represents a serious "degradation" of its performance requirements. Despite such internal evidence, the report stated, "An extensive evaluation by Air Force and NASA experts has revealed no major design deficiencies in the aircraft or engines, and there is a high probability that all range, payload, takeoff and landing performance requirements will be met." [10]

In contrast to the report's rosy summary, anyone who bothered to read the entire document found several other indications that all was not well with the C–5A. According to the report, "the schedule for completion of tests and demonstrations appears optimistic." The reason for this appeared elsewhere in the report. It mentioned certain "areas in which problems could arise," such as subsystem integration, subsystem reliability, and structural fatigue. In these vague indications of potential problems, the Whittaker Report proved remarkably prophetic.

On July 13, 1969, two weeks before the Air Force officially released the Whittaker Report to the press, a C–5A undergoing static ground tests, designed to simulate flight conditions, developed a rather serious "structural fatigue" problem — its wing cracked. The Air Force and Lockheed hastily announced that the crack occurred at 128 per cent of its design load limit, or 28 per cent more than the normal maximum load.[11] An Air Force colonel even told the House Military Construction Subcommittee that the wing failure was deliberate: "The reason the wing came off this aircraft is because we meant for it to come off." [12] No one laughed.

Despite such crude attempts to cover up the meaning of the wing crack, people in the aircraft industry were fully aware of its significance. The C–5A contract called for the plane to demon-

strate an ability to fly while carrying 50 per cent more weight
than its normal load limit. Even this requirement is not particularly severe. As a normal safety precaution, the Federal
Aviation Authority requires commercial passenger planes about
to begin service to demonstrate a design strength 100 per cent
above their legal load limits. The Air Force had originally
planned to have the C–5A meet the tougher FAA regulations, as
its C–141 and most military transports do, but later decided
against the idea.

Lockheed and Air Force technicians quickly designed a "wing
fix" which they announced would be "retro-fitted" to the C–5As
already built, or under construction. This would supposedly
solve the wing problem. It didn't. Two months later, in September, 1969, the wing fix "failed" in a ground test at only 83 per cent
of the plane's load limit. This the Air Force did not announce.
The public only learned about it because Representative Otis Pike
happened to hear of it in the bar of a Beverly Hills, California,
hotel where the Society of Experimental Test Pilots was holding
its annual meeting. When he returned to Washington, Pike questioned the Air Force about the second wing crack. At first, the
replies he received ran something along the lines of "Wing crack?
What wing crack?" After repeated queries, however, USAF
officials finally admitted the failure, but told Pike they were "not
too concerned about it." [13] Wondering about the possible cost on
any wing fix, Senator Proxmire repeatedly asked the Air Force
whether the government was liable for the repair costs on the
wing. He received what he called "a lot of gobbledygook back,
but no satisfactory response." [14]

During the Senate and House debates on the C–5A that fall,
nearly every speaker seemed to feel that the plane was unassaila-
ble in terms of performance. Surprisingly, however, two of the
plane's defenders did give some hints that it might be having some

difficulties. Senator Goldwater conceded that while "initial tests have been encouraging, normal development problems have been encountered." [15] Senator Cannon told his colleagues the Air Force and DoD had assured him that when delivered, the C–5A "will meet most if not all the operational requirements laid down for it." [16] Senator Stennis referred to the cracked wing, but claimed such events "nearly always happen in testing," and that it occurred "well over the expected limits." [17] (It had not, but no one argued the point.)

In the short time allotted by the House for discussion of the C–5A, Otis Pike described the two wing failures and pointed out that contrary to statements by the Air Force and Lockheed, the wing fix would be a complex matter. "I do not say that Lockheed can not fix them," Pike said, "but we do not have the slightest idea how long it is going to take, and we do not have the slightest idea how much it is going to cost." [18]

In the speech that he was unable to give in the 75 seconds allowed him during that debate, Congressman Moorhead stated that he was "more than a little dubious" about the entire question of the C–5A's quality. The Air Force, said Moorhead, has been issuing "glowing reports" claiming that the C–5A was an excellent airplane. "But is it?" he asked his fellow representatives. "Do you know? I certainly do not." He recalled that in June, the Air Force had agreed to supply the Subcommittee on Economy in Government with a list of all the contract changes affecting the plane's performance. Four months later the subcommittee was still waiting. Intrigued by this reticence, Moorhead himself requested the information and also got a run-around from the Air Force. Finally he was forced to ask the General Accounting Office to get the information for him.

"Why should they avoid responding?" Moorhead wondered. "It is not a question of security classification. It is not a question of time. They have had almost four months to reply. In view of their past practice of withholding bad news from the Congress, I am becoming more and more suspicious all the time that we may end up with a plane which does indeed fly, but one which must be flown so gingerly that it will be of little utility . . . Why else would they refuse to supply us this information? It would be the height of irony if we were to end up with a complete fiasco on this program — a fantastically priced plane that barely works, and which we do not really need." [19]

Two months later, in December, 1969, when he learned the Air Force planned to formally accept the first C–5A despite its still uncorrected wing problem, Moorhead charged that the plane would endanger the lives of the training crews scheduled to fly it. Suggesting that the hasty delivery was designed to save Lockheed further penalty payments for schedule slippage, he urged Air Force Secretary Seamans to defer acceptance and delivery until the structural defects were solved. "It would be a charade on the American people," said Moorhead, "for the Air Force to accept the plane, then send it back to fix the defects." Seamans replied that he had "every confidence" in the C–5A and assured Moorhead the planes would be flown under strict weight limitations until Lockheed completed the wing fix.[20]

Later that week the GAO finally sent Moorhead the results of its investigation into the C–5A's performance problems. According to the GAO report, Moorhead had been correct in guessing the Air Force had something to hide. It listed 25 defects, ranging from relatively minor and easily solved items, such as a faulty signal light for the nose landing gear, to a number of more serious problems:[21]

1. As a result of the wing failure, the plane's load limit had been reduced to 100,000 pounds—less than half its maximum capacity.
2. Because of failures with engine mounts, the throttles could not

be opened fully, which meant the plane could not take off from unimproved runways, or fly at full speed.

3. The plane's maximum speed had also been severely restricted by design problems with the wing ailerons.

4. Problems with the landing gear were preventing the plane from making crosswind landings, and from "kneeling" to load cargo.

5. The radar system, the altimeter, and the automatic pilot were not functioning properly.

Although Lockheed later protested that it had not yet completed tests on many of these defective items, this only gave further evidence that the C–5A was still not ready for delivery.

Moorhead released this GAO report two days before the scheduled delivery of the first C–5A, accusing the Air Force of accepting an "inferior" and "substandard" plane. "We were told it could do all sorts of marvelous things," said Moorhead. "How many of these marvelous things can the C–5A do? Not one. As of now, it can not do one of them. As of right now, the C–5A has been so severely restricted that it cannot land or take off from a rough field at all. So the 'remote presence' that was so highly touted to us in Congress a few months ago is more remote than we were led to believe." (Due to the C–5A's structural limitations, the Pentagon, in 1971, is no longer claiming the plane has the capability to land on "unimproved," i.e., dirt, or even "unpaved" runways. The term now used is "lightly paved.")

Moorhead urged the Air Force to delay its acceptance of the C–5As until a study could show the relative cost of a production delay rather than bring the unfixed planes back to Marietta for repairs and modifications. He pointed out that the "retro-fit" of the wing supports alone involved disassembling the wings and making 11 structural changes to each one. Moorhead had asked the GAO to check on the cost of this "fix," the GAO asked the Air Force, and the Air Force had asked Lockheed. No one really knew.[22]

Despite the unanswered questions, the Air Force took delivery of the first C–5A with most of its 25 defects still defective. On December 17, 1969, the sixty-sixth anniversary of the Wright brothers' flight at Kitty Hawk, North Carolina, an Air Force crew flew the plane from the Lockheed-Georgia plant in Marietta to a welcome celebration at Altus Air Force Base in Oklahoma. Accepting this first C–5A for the Air Force at Marietta, General James Ferguson, Commander of the Air Force Systems Command, called it "an exceedingly versatile instrument of national policy." Claiming the plane represents "a genuine revolution in aeronautics," General Ferguson praised Lockheed and its subcontractors for their "great achievement."

In January, 1970, four weeks after the acceptance ceremonies, another C–5A undergoing flight tests at Marietta developed a ten-inch crack in exactly the same point in its wing where the earlier cracks had occurred. This time the Air Force grounded all C–5As, "pending completion of precautionary inspections." A spokesman for Lockheed explained that this latest crack had occurred on a plane that had undergone "strenuous testing . . . performing far more than it will ever be expected to do." This was not completely true. Neither this plane nor any of the other operational C–5As had yet demonstrated the ability to fly with 150 per cent of their normal load limit, as the contract called for.[23]

After an "ultrasonic" examination of the 11 C–5As already built, the Air Force cleared eight of them for flying, again with a severely restricted cargo load. At a Pentagon press briefing, the Air Force claimed the restrictions would not hamper its use of the C–5As already delivered for crew training, and that if the wing modification proved successful, the plane's cargo-carrying ability would not be affected. This was the first time the Air Force had implied a possibility that the wing fix might not work. Reporters who asked about a rumor that the latest crack had occurred on a plane *with* the wing fix received "no comment."[24]

By the end of January, 1970, the Air Force did have some idea about the cost of the wing fix. It would involve 240 pounds of aluminum bracings to be added to each of the aircraft already built or then under construction, and to be built into those not yet under construction. The cost would run about $80,000 apiece, or $6.5 million extra for all 81 planes. Six months later, like all cost estimates on the C–5A, this one had grown to $185,000 per plane, bringing the total estimate for wing repair on all the planes to $15 million. The Air Force said Lockheed would have to absorb these costs on the first 58 planes. But because of the complexities of the contract's repricing formula, it was not clear who would have to pay for the modification costs on the remaining 23 planes of the fourth squadron.

Official reports from Lockheed headquarters in California during this period carried little comment about the C–5A's troubles. Lockheed's 1969 annual report issued in the spring of 1970, assured stockholders that the C–5A was "meeting or exceeding performance guarantees." General Ferguson told the SASC in March, 1970, he was "highly confident at this time that the C–5A will generally meet or exceed all operational requirements." Under questioning, however, General Ferguson admitted that Lockheed's chance of meeting its current delivery schedule was "highly improbable" because the wing fix was still not fixed and the sophisticated multi-mode radar system was still functioning with "lower than desired reliability." [25]

In an attempt to allay the controversy caused by the January wing failure, the Air Force announced the creation of another "blue ribbon" outside panel of aerodynamics experts to review the C–5A's technical problems. To give the new panel badly needed prestige, the Air Force picked as its head, Raymond Bisplinghoff, dean of engineering at Massachusetts Institute of Technology. Despite the difficulty of pronouncing it, Bisplinghoff's name was dropped frequently during the following months by the C–5A's defenders. In March, Air Force Secretary Seamans told the HASC: "It is our belief, based on the preliminary judgment of Dr. Bisplinghoff and the people he has with him, that Lockheed has a good solution to the problem." [26] When Mendel Rivers needed support in ramming an extra $200 million appropriation for the C–5A through the House in April, he made a special point of telling everyone he had personally inspected the plane "with one of our great aircraft engineers, Dr. Raymond Bisplinghoff, of the Mass. Institute of Technology. I did not want to trust my layman's impression." [27] The legislators naturally assumed Dr. Bisplinghoff's professional opinion of the C–5A was as enthusiastically favorable as that of chairman Rivers.

Those who recalled the whitewash produced by the Whittaker Report nearly one year before did not expect much from this new investigation, despite the eminence of its leader. This time, however, something went wrong — or right, depending on one's point of view. The Bisplinghoff review panel made an oral report to Secretary Seamans early in May, 1970, with the full written report due in mid-June. A few weeks after the private conference in Seaman's office, enough of what transpired leaked out to make any cover-up difficult.

According to a report first published in the highly authoritative *Armed Forces Journal,* the Bisplinghoff panel found that because of the C–5A's many structural problems, its fatigue life would only reach one fourth of the 30,000-hour requirement set for it by the Military Airlift Command. The panel reportedly told Seamans that probably no possible wing fix could strengthen the existing wing enough to meet this fatigue life requirement and that the Air Force should consider designing an entirely new wing.[28]

From a series of Air Force and Lockheed press releases that followed this premature disclosure, it became clear that the C–5A's fatigue life problem was not completely Lockheed's fault.

The performance specifications given Lockheed in 1965 by the Air Force Systems Command did not match the 1970 requirements of the Military Airlift Command, which would operate the planes. Thus, even if Lockheed did eventually produce a plane that met its contract specifications (which by this time seemed highly unlikely), it would have still fallen far short of MAC standards. Either MAC's standards had changed considerably between 1965 and 1970 — in which case someone should have informed the Air Force and Lockheed — or else the Air Force had never bothered checking its specifications with MAC in the first place, a possibility which those familiar with the Pentagon's bureaucracy consider entirely reasonable.

No one really knows how much of the findings of the Bisplinghoff review would have become public if the panel's oral report had not leaked out. For even after the leak, the Pentagon and its friends on Capitol Hill tried to cover things up. Mendel Rivers called the public reports of the C–5A's structural inadequacies "pure speculation" and accused the press of "irresponsible charges and allegations." [29] Deputy Secretary Packard, who was briefing the SASC when the story broke, admitted the C–5A had technical problems with its wing, landing gear, and electronic systems, but assured the committee the Air Force and Lockheed would work out a "satisfactory" solution to these problems. For technical and financial reasons, however, he conceded that "it is probably not possible at this time to hold the contractor responsible to meet all of the contract specifications." [30]

A few weeks later, in June, 1970, Air Force Secretary Seamans called a Pentagon press conference to issue an official summary of the findings of the Bisplinghoff panel, with the full report to be released the following day. The effect of this maneuver was that the Pentagon's bland official summary took up whatever space the news media devoted to the story. The Air Force

Public Affairs Office correctly assumed that few reporters would
bother to read the full report the next day, and that almost no
papers would run a second story on the review panel's findings.[31]

According to Seamans, the panel had merely recommended
further fatigue testing on the C-5A's wing. "We do not require a
new wing for this airplane," he insisted. Pressed on this point by
reporters who recalled the earlier leaked version of the panel's
oral briefing, Seamans backed off a bit, saying that a major redesign of the wing was "very unlikely." The official summary
only stated that "additional modifications to the wing structure in
conjunction with other measures will be required in order to
provide an operationally useful vehicle." Seamans said the cost
of the required changes and other measures would be "very minor
compared to the overall cost" of the program. Considering that
the estimated cost of the program at that time was somewhere
between $4 and $5 billion, one might well wonder just what sum
Seamans would call minor.

According to Seamans, the Bisplinghoff Report only "points
out what we already knew — that we do have difficulties with the
aircraft." If the Air Force did indeed already know what the
Bisplinghoff panel learned (and there is good reason to suspect
it did), it certainly had kept this knowledge a secret from Congress, which was just then preparing to authorize additional funds
to pay for the plane. Seamans said the report reaffirmed his
conviction that the C-5A "can perform the primary mission for
which it was built" and hoped its release would encourage Congress to come up with a few hundred million dollars more for the
program. Lockheed-Georgia's new president, Robert Fuhrman,
hailed the report as proof that the C-5A would not need a new
wing. "The important thing," said Fuhrman, "is that the basic
design and structure of the C-5 are sound."[32]

One might well wonder just what report Fuhrman and Seamans

had been reading that led them to make such cheerful statements. Anyone who bothered to read Bisplinghoff's report would have hardly found it heartening. In addition to its implication that the wing would require at least serious modification, it noted that many of the plane's electronic functions would not be operational for "a considerable time to come": the automatic flight control system would not be complete for almost another year; the plane could still not execute its vital all-weather landings on unpaved fields; the navigation system had "experienced difficulties"; the sophisticated multi-mode radar system had performed so poorly the panel recommended dropping it entirely, replacing it with a less complex commercially available system. The best the Bisplinghoff Report could muster in conclusion was that if Lockheed solved all these problems, and made the required modifications, the C–5A would be less versatile than originally planned, but still "very useful."

Because of its many defects, the C–5A was proving extremely useful in providing emergency training for the flight and ground crews out at Altus Air Force Base. In May, 1970, for example, a C–5A undergoing test flights at Altus developed a problem with its pressurization system, necessitating a speedy descent and an emergency landing. The landing proved too much for the 28-wheel landing gear, which partially collapsed upon impact.

On June 6, 1970, a crowd of military and civilian officials, including Mendel Rivers, gathered at Charleston Air Force Base to celebrate the arrival of the first "operational" C–5A. As the plane touched down, one tire blew out upon the impact and another wheel departed from the landing gear completely, bouncing down the runway by itself, to the delight of the TV cameramen covering the event. As the plane continued to taxi in, one quick-witted Air Force public information officer told nearby newsmen, "Don't worry, its got 26 tires left." The pilot, MAC Commander,

General Jack Catton, later explained the mishap as best he could. "The lock washer came off," he told reporters, "and a lock nut unscrewed, causing the wheel to fall off. What we don't know is why the washer came off." [33]

While the plane itself suffered no damage from this incident, the public nature of this latest fiasco marred the day's festivities. It also dealt a blow to the pride of the Air Force and Charleston, both institutions dear to the heart of Charleston's favorite son, Mendel Rivers. As he recovered his composure after the landing, he muttered, "Some people would rather have seen a wing fall off than a tire. All I can say is to hell with them." [34]

Four months later, on October 17, 1970, the first C–5A to fly, which had since been delivered to the Air Force and then returned to Lockheed-Georgia for "further testing," developed a leak in a fuel cell. At 1:17 A.M. on a Saturday morning, while undergoing something called "fuel-cell purging" on the flight line, the plane caught fire and exploded, killing one mechanic and injuring another. It burned for more than two hours, requiring all the resources of Lockheed's flight line fire trucks, plus the help of units from Marietta and nearby communities before finally being extinguished.

Reporters who watched all that money going up in smoke were told later by Lockheed spokesmen that the plane was "worth $23 million." Since the Air Force was then estimating the total cost of the 81-plane C–5A program at about $5 billion, or roughly $60 million per plane, that $23 million figure was probably just a mistake. If not, it represented an unwittingly candid disclosure by Lockheed that the $60 million C–5As are in fact only worth $23 million.

CHAPTER THIRTEEN
Stock Market Implications

" . . . the nature of the estimates was such that if publicly disclosed they might put Lockheed's position in the common market in jeopardy."

Colonel Kenneth Beckman,
Director of the C–5 System Program Office

THROUGHOUT the entire C–5A affair, few critics had accused Air Force or Lockheed officials of anything worse than sloppy management. Even those who did claim the Air Force or Lockheed had deliberately deceived Congress and the public, by concealing the plane's cost and technical problems, generally assumed the motive for this deception was simply the normal tendency of any bureaucracy to cover up its failures. No one had ever suggested that such behavior might be tainted by anything worse.

From time to time, however, those who followed the C–5A story detected the odor of a major scandal involving Lockheed's stock. The first whiff came during the April, 1969, hearings of the Military Operations Subcommittee, with the testimony of Colonel Kenneth Beckman, Director of the Air Force's C–5 System Program Office. When the subcommittee's counsel Herbert Roback asked him why the cost overrun estimates had been "left out" of official reports on the C–5A program, Colonel Beckman nervously gave the first hint that the Air Force's concealment of the overrun represented more than just an attempt to protect the Air Force: "Because of the nature of the overrun, we felt . . . that the projections we were making were actually estimates,

subject to actual proof later on, and that the nature of the estimates was such that if publicly disclosed they might put Lockheed's position in the common market in jeopardy."

Mr. Roback asked if the Air Force made it a common practice
to conceal cost overruns because "the contractor is liable to go
under on the market." Colonel Beckman, by now probably aware
that he had slipped badly, could only mumble, "I can not say for
sure, sir." When Representative Moorhead asked Colonel Beckman if by "common market" he meant the stock market, the
colonel quickly claimed he only meant "the general market . . .
the commercial market." [1] Moorhead smelled something, however, and asked his staff aide, Peter Stockton, to do some research
in the files of the Securities & Exchange Commission on Lockheed's stock during the time of the C–5A contract. Senator
Proxmire, when he heard of Colonel Beckman's testimony, called
on the SEC to launch its own investigation into the matter.

During the House Armed Services Committee hearings several
weeks later, Representative Otis Pike raised the "question that
bothered me most about the C–5A contract, and that is the fact
that they [the Air Force] apparently concealed a lot of these
figures, and they concealed these cost overruns to protect Lockheed's position either on the stock market, or because they were
about to issue a debenture." [2] Even HASC chairman Mendel
Rivers seemed concerned about this matter. He asked Air Force
Secretary Seamans, "Can't you find out who in the Air Force had
concern for Lockheed's corporate interests on the stock market?"
Seamans dutifully promised to find out, and Rivers told him,
"Whoever that was, I don't think he ought to be in this job over
there." [3] He soon wasn't. Colonel Beckman had named Assistant
Secretary Robert Charles as the man who ordered the cost overrun
information deleted, and soon afterward the Pentagon announced
the departure of Mr. Charles.

At his farewell press conference in May, 1969, Charles conceded that in deciding to withhold information of the C–5A cost overrun, the potentially adverse effect of such news on Lockheed's stock had indeed been "a factor," but an "extraordinarily minor" one.[4] However, the C–5 System Program Office, which received his order to delete certain cost information on the program, apparently had a different view of the importance of this stock factor. In its April–June, 1968, report, the SPO referred to its estimates of Lockheed's over-ceiling costs on the C–5A and cautioned: "The SPO has treated this information as extremely sensitive in view of adverse publicity and stock market implications." [5]

When Lockheed board chairman Daniel Haughton appeared before the Senate Armed Services Committee in June, 1969, he specifically denied that either Lockheed or the Air Force had suppressed or concealed information on the C–5A cost overrun in order to protect the company's stock.[6] (According to a later investigation both Haughton and Charles did try to talk the SPO out of issuing the February, 1967, cure notice to Lockheed, but the SPO refused to give in and sent it anyway.[7])

Three months later, in September, 1969, Moorhead released the results of his research into the files of the SEC, and the smell of scandal became unmistakable. Between November, 1965, and January, 1966, just after Lockheed had won the C–5A contract, six of the company's top officers sold a total of 11,742 shares of their own Lockheed stock for more than $700,000.[8] Now the average Lockheed stockholder at the time would have reasonably assumed that the C–5A contract, supposedly worth about $2 billion, assured the company of continued prosperity, and that its stock was therefore a sound investment. As a result of such optimism among the general public, the price of Lockheed's stock had risen to $60 on the news of the contract award. Such pessimism on the part of the company's senior officers would have amazed these ordinary stockholders. Their action does seem strange, unless, of course, those officials knew something the average Lockheed stockholder didn't. Now it is conceivable that they all just happened to need immediate cash at the same time, which, as we shall see, was their own explanation. Or they may have felt that the good news was sufficiently reflected in the price of the stock for the time being. But they also might have known their winning bid on the C-5A contract was so low that the company might lose money on it.

Somebody seems to have known something else about a year later. Between January and March, 1967, with the price of stock still above $60 per share, ten Lockheed executives decided to sell another 10,403 shares worth about $700,000.[9] Since such men do not usually rise to corporate eminence through stupidity, one again must assume they had some reason for their simultaneous sellout. This time the reason could well have been two letters (December, 1966, and January, 1967) from the Air Force, warning Lockheed that the C-5A program was in serious trouble. So serious in fact, that in February the Air Force delivered a formal "cure notice" threatening to "terminate" the contract for "default" unless the company quickly solved its technical and cost problems on the C-5A.

The facts uncovered by Moorhead raised serious implications of what is commonly called "insider trading." Federal law specifically prohibits corporate officials from trading in the stock of their own company on the basis of "inside" information about the company's affairs that is unavailable to other stockholders and that might affect the price of the company's stock. The law requires that such officials report to the SEC any sales or purchases of their own company's stock. This insider trading law was purposely designed to protect the general public from the sort of thing which may have happened to thousands of Lockheed stock-holders.

The fact that these executives sold their stock in Lockheed does not in itself represent any violation of SEC regulations. But if they did so on the basis of inside information unavailable to other Lockheed stockholders, it does. Since the C–5A contract was the largest Lockheed had at the time — for several years it brought in about 25 per cent of all corporate revenues — one might expect these senior executives to have been informed about the program's troubles. They certainly must have been better informed than the rest of Lockheed's stockholders, who only learned of the $2 billion cost overrun along with the rest of the public when Fitz-gerald confirmed it before the Proxmire subcommittee nearly two years later.

In releasing his findings, Moorhead said "these sell-offs might be connected to inside knowledge" of the C–5A's problems and "fear of public disclosure." [10] While he emphasized carefully that he was not accusing anyone of breaking the law, he did call on the SEC to determine whether the Lockheed officials violated the law against insider trading. Asked what they would do with the information uncovered by Moorhead, SEC officials simply said it would be "incorporated" into their study of Lockheed and the C–5A.

Lockheed, of course, denied everything. The company's Bur-bank, California, headquarters issued a statement claiming that the facts released by Moorhead had all been reported as required to the SEC, and since the commission's investigation called for by Proxmire was still pending, the company felt "it would be im-proper to discuss individual involvement." [11] While this may have pleased the individual officials involved, it did not do much for the rest of the company's stockholders, who were understandably bitter. For while some of their company's top officials were selling out near the stock's high, at prices ranging from $60 to $70 a share, less fortunate souls, not privy to the inside view of the C–5A program, were holding on to their Lockheed stock, or even buying more. Those who held on watched it fall from a high of $73 a share in 1967 down to $30 in the summer of 1969, after the publicity resulting from the congressional hearings. Since then, outpacing the market's general decline, the stock has fallen as low as $7 a share.

Like all laws designed to protect the public, the effect of the law prohibiting insider trading depends upon the rigor of its enforcement, which is left to the SEC. Since the members of the SEC are political appointees, with the financial interests and prejudices common to most men of affairs, the commission has never been noted for vigorous enforcement of any laws that might do serious damage to a major company such as Lockheed. Since Moorhead's figures had been lying around in the SEC's own files for several years, one can only wonder how long they would have continued to lie there undisturbed by the SEC if he had not looked for them.

Fortunately for the public, individual stockholders who find themselves unprotected by the SEC can turn to the federal courts for help in settling claims against companies they feel have wronged them. With the disclosure that top Lockheed officials had dumped more than $1.4 million worth of their stock in the company at higher prices, many of those who held on when the stock plummeted felt they had been taken for a ride. Some of them sought redress. A New York attorney named Richard Stull filed suit in May, 1969, charging the company and its officials with concealing the C–5A cost overrun from their stockholders in order to "artificially inflate the market price" of Lockheed stock. The suit also alleged that Arthur Young & Company, Lockheed's accountants, "aided and abetted" the company's management in this affair by omitting the losses on the C–5A from their accounting reports to the stockholders.[12] (Lockheed and Arthur Young & Company have denied the charges in Stull's suit.)

Other suits brought out further accusations concerning the company's stock. In March, 1967, in order to raise some liquid capital (probably to help cover the growing losses on the C–5A) Lockheed offered for public sale $125 million in convertible debentures — $1000 bonds paying 4½ per cent interest. The prospectus accompanying this issue told prospective buyers the C–5A program was "not in danger" and that "Lockheed is confident that it will be able to perform [the contract] satisfactorily." [13] Now reasonable men might well have wondered about Lockheed's confidence in the C–5A program had they known that between January and March, 1967, ten top Lockheed executives had unloaded much of their own stock in the company.[14] Since that information was not generally known at the time, however, the debenture issue found a ready market and was fully subscribed.

Among the purchasers was Colonial Realty, a small Pennsylvania investment company which bought 105 of the bonds for $105,000. Like the rest of the Lockheed stockholders, Colonial only learned of the C–5A's serious troubles two years later, when it read the press coverage of the congressional hearings in May, 1969. By then, the price of the bonds had fallen off sharply. By September, they were selling at just over $500 each — a 50 per cent drop in value. Soon after Moorhead disclosed how Lockheed executives had been dumping their own stock at the time, Colonial Realty filed suit charging Lockheed with illegally concealing its troubles with the C–5A program in order to create a more favorable market for its debenture issue. Colonial claimed it had bought the bonds on the basis of the prospectus and that the prospectus was "false and misleading, contained misrepresenta-

tions, and failed to disclose material facts" about the C–5A cost
overrun. The suit also charges that Lockheed officials who signed
the prospectus knew it was misleading and engaged in a "scheme
to defraud investors." [15]

In a formal reply, Lockheed "vigorously" denied the charges in
this suit, insisting that its registration statement filed with the SEC
for the debenture issue "represented whole and accurate disclosure
of all material information." [16] One crucial point here was obviously who decided which information was "material." The prospectus clearly gave the impression that, despite some problems,
Lockheed and the Air Force had reached a satisfactory agreement on the C–5A program.

Those who attended the hearings of the Military Operations
Subcommittee in April, 1969, may have recalled a memo submitted by Representative Moorhead that sheds some curious light on
the nature of this "agreement" between Lockheed and the Air
Force. In the memo to Harold Brown, then Secretary of the Air
Force, Assistant Secretary Robert Charles noted Lockheed's plans
to issue the debentures. He told Brown that news of the Air Force
cure notice "may cause concern, particularly in the financial community, that the C–5 is in serious trouble, particularly if they
ascertain that cure notices have not been issued on other major
programs such as the F–111, including some that were in fact
terminated." [17] Perhaps in response to Charles' concern, the C–5
System Program Office, which had prepared a press release on
the cure notice, never released it to the press.[18]

The Charles memo, Moorhead's discoveries, and other tidbits
of information were all supposedly under investigation by the
SEC, but nothing seemed to be happening. Reporters who called
after six months to inquire about the results of the investigation
were simply told it was not yet completed. "We're not like the
FBI, you know," an SEC spokesman explained. "We don't have

unlimited resources. We're lucky if we can put one or two men on these things."

A shortage of manpower was probably the least of the impediments blocking the SEC from taking vigorous action in the Lockheed scandal. The SEC staff, in fact, had conducted an extremely thorough investigation, combing through hundreds of documents and taking testimony from most of the people involved in the C–5A affair. The Air Force was not always helpful. When the SEC called Fitzgerald to testify, the Air Force sent an official along to sit in on his interview, but the SEC men told him to leave.

When the investigation was finished, rumors began to spread around Washington that charges would be brought against several Lockheed executives for insider trading and failure to disclose information. According to the rumors, the SEC would also recommend bringing charges against certain Air Force officials for conspiring to conceal the cost overrun on the C–5A in order to protect Lockheed. About the same time these rumors were circulating, some of the young SEC staff lawyers leaked word to the press that their efforts to press charges were being blocked by "higher authority." [19] SEC chairman Hamer Budge denied all the rumors.

To anyone familiar with Washington politics, the possibility of White House interest in the Lockheed case is perfectly reasonable. After all, Lockheed has impressive Republican credentials: its directors and officers contributed a total of $38,880 to the GOP campaign in 1968. (Lockheed was not alone in its generosity. Officials of the country's largest defense and space contractors contributed a total of $1,235,402 to GOP campaigns in 1968.[20]) Now no administration would want to cause unnecessary trouble for such loyal friends, and the White House has ample power to protect its friends in such matters. First of all, the SEC commissioners are appointed by the President, and their terms of office are renewable at his discretion. And even if the SEC did recommend that charges be brought against Lockheed officials, the Justice Department, headed by the President's close friend, Attorney General John Mitchell, would make the final decision and handle the prosecution.

In June, 1970, more than a year after its investigation began, the SEC announced in a terse 70-word statement that its study of "the Lockheed matter" had "not disclosed evidence of unlawful insider trading" and that no charges would be brought. Senator Proxmire and Representative Moorhead called this outcome "disappointing," although they did not seem particularly surprised. A Lockheed spokesman in Burbank said the corporation was "gratified that the SEC's announcement appears to give Lockheed officials a clean bill of health . . . We expected no less." [21]

While the SEC commissioners officially found "no evidence" of illegal insider trading, anyone reading the staff report of the investigation (released only after pressure from Congress) would hardly call it "a clean bill of health." Citing specific instances of heavy selling by top Lockheed officials, the report raised "the possibility that this was done on the basis of inside information." [22]

The SEC investigation confirmed that the heavy selling of Lockheed stock by top corporate officials came in two distinct periods — November, 1965, through January, 1966, and January, 1967, through March, 1967. At no other times during the four years following the signing of the C-5A contract was there any comparable amount of selling by Lockheed officials. [23] By far the most active month of selling came in January, 1967, just before the Air Force sent Lockheed the cure notice on February 1. In that month alone, six top Lockheed officials unloaded nearly 8000 shares of Lockheed stock. [24]

All the Lockheed officials investigated by the SEC denied emphatically that their sales of stock had been based on any inside knowledge of cost problems in the C–5A program. Each had a perfectly plausible explanation for selling $100,000 or so worth of Lockheed stock when he did: buying a house, buying land, paying off loans, etc. Several used the money to reduce loans as big as $200,000 from the Lockheed Credit Union. On January 23 and 24, just one week before the cure notice, A. Carl Kotchian, president of the Lockheed Aircraft Corporation, sold 2004 shares, in order to make payments on an alfalfa ranch.[25] On January 9, three weeks before the cure notice, Thomas May, then C–5A program manager at Lockheed-Georgia, sold 2200 shares of Lockheed stock for $135,292, in order to buy a house.[26]

Of all the explanations by Lockheed executives who sold substantial amounts of stock during this period, the one that troubled the SEC investigators most was that of Mr. May. His sale of 2200 shares — more than 75 per cent of his entire holdings of Lockheed stock — was the only sale he made during the four years studied by the SEC.[27] Noting that this sale came after a warning letter from the Air Force, and just before the cure notice, the SEC report commented: "It is obvious that he, more so than any of the other insiders who sold Lockheed stock, was aware of the exact condition of the C–5A at different stages in its development. He would have been privy to all the reports and information disseminated in connection with the project. Because of his past experience on the C–130 and C–141 programs, he was in an excellent position to evaluate the seriousness of the problems which did develop on the C–5A." [28]

Like the other Lockheed executives, May insisted his decision to sell was unrelated to any inside information on the C–5A program's troubles. However, referring to May's statement that he sold the stock in order to finance the purchase of a house, the SEC report commented delicately, "we are not entirely satisfied with his explanation," [29] pointing out that he sold the stock "before any binding contract was signed, and before he had even found the home he eventually bought." [30]

In addition to the law prohibiting insider trading, federal statutes require corporations to make clear and full disclosure to their stockholders of corporate activities that might affect the price of the company's stock. Certainly disclosure of the extent to which the C-5A program was running into financial and technical problems would have affected the price of Lockheed stock. Yet after studying the history of the C-5A program in great detail, and comparing this information with Lockheed's annual and interim reports to its stockholders during this period, the SEC investigators found many problems they described as "apparent at the time of each report," that were not disclosed.[31] "From the Commission's point of view," the SEC Report stated, "there is a question as to the adequacy of disclosure in annual and interim filings with the Commission, and with the [New York Stock] Exchange, as well as information prepared for public distribution." [32]

The SEC Report offers considerable evidence that Lockheed was aware of the serious cost problems on the C-5A program before the company informed its stockholders about them. By March, 1967, the Air Force C-5 System Program Office had notified Lockheed that its estimates already showed a potential $250 million overrun on the program. Lockheed questioned the accuracy of the Air Force figures, but the SPO's chief financial officer, who gave the figures to Lockheed, told board chairman Haughton that even the Air Force figures were probably low.[33] Although the budgets on the C-5A program were revised upward several times by Lockheed-Georgia, a September, 1967, report from that division to corporate headquarters in California warned: "we are more than a little concerned about our ability to perform to Project Budget No. 4." [34] By the end of 1967, Lockheed-

Georgia's chief financial officer assigned to the C–5A program reported to corporate headquarters: "I'm not trying to paint a gloomy picture, but the fact of the matter is that we *do* have some very real cost hazards, and they're not exactly minor in nature." His estimate put these cost "hazards" at $260 million.[35] In May, 1968, an Air Force C–5 SPO report noted: "We believe Lockheed recognized that they are in real trouble from the standpoint of cost about the first of the year." [36]

Despite all these indications that Lockheed was well aware of the serious cost problems developing on the C–5A program during 1967, there was no mention of them in Lockheed's mid-1967 report to stockholders, no mention of them in the annual report for 1967, and no mention of them in a semi-annual report sent out in July, 1968. Only in the 1968 Annual Report, issued in the spring of 1969 (after Fitzgerald had testified about the $2 billion cost overrun) did Lockheed finally imply the existence of any problems, stating: "no loss is anticipated on the contract." Even the Air Force at this point was estimating that Lockheed would lose several hundred million dollars on the C–5A.[37]

Referring to Lockheed's March, 1967, prospectus for the convertible debenture issue, the SEC Report commented:

> While there was a very general disclosure . . . the statements made did not fully and adequately describe all pertinent factors, and it requires much reading between the lines, with knowledge of the underlying circumstances, to catch the issues and the real risks facing this company. There is also a substantial question as to whether the "cure notice" itself is adequately described. While the information is basically included in the prospectus, it is included in two widely separated sections, which makes it difficult to comprehend the full implications.
>
> In addition to this, there was no mention made in the prospectus of the various contractual factors which had substantially increased the risk on this contract, of the technical problems and

related cost overruns which had been experienced to date, of cost increases in the subcontract area . . . of increases in labor and overhead rates over those projected initially, of schedule uncertainties which had developed, of the fact that not only had the engineering task been underestimated, but that similar problems were appearing in tooling, and that there was concern that the same factor might develop in production. No indication was given of financial problems which had already been admitted, as reflected in the budget overruns on work to date and the very substantial recent increase in budget . . .[38]

If the Justice Department did not find sufficient grounds in the report of the SEC investigation to bring charges for illegal insider trading, or failure to disclose pertinent information, it might well have considered prosecution under Title 18, Chapter 47, Section 1001, of the U.S. Criminal Code, which provides for up to five years in jail for anyone who "in any matter within the jurisdiction of any department or agency of the United States knowingly or willfully . . . conceals . . . a material fact." In a memo written as early as November, 1966, after Lockheed refused to cooperate with cost analysts from his office, USAF Assistant Secretary for Financial Management Leonard Marks complained of a "visibility" problem regarding Lockheed's cost data on the C–5A: "It appears that Lockheed is holding back full disclosure of the information generated by their own systems." [39] Two years later, in May, 1968, the Air Force C–5 System Program Office complained that since the beginning of that year Lockheed had been "attempting to limit our visibility on program costs." [40]

To a layman, this all sounds very much like willful concealment of material facts from the Air Force, a federal agency. The trouble with bringing charges against Lockheed for concealment, however, is that such action might have reflected unflatteringly upon certain Air Force officials, who certainly did as much concealing of the C–5A cost information as did Lockheed officials.

Fitzgerald had complained about this problem of Air Force concealment for nearly two years, and the House Military Operations Subcommittee had already disclosed that the C–5 System Program Office had been ordered to omit the cost overrun from its reports. Any court investigation into the C–5A affair therefore would have been unpleasant for the United States Air Force as well as for Lockheed.

Perhaps as an attempt to satisfy those who had been expecting some action as a result of the SEC investigation, the commission announced it would hold public hearings on the whole question of financial disclosure by major defense contractors. However, shortly after these hearings opened in July, 1970, they were forced into "indefinite" adjournment when lawyers for Lockheed objected to the release of the 3700 pages of testimony and other material gathered by the SEC investigators during their study of Lockheed. Lockheed's lawyers claimed much of this material was "irrelevant, inappropriate, and confidential." [41]

CHAPTER FOURTEEN

A Small Matter of $500 Million

". . . there is no question about the need to preserve this important capability which Lockheed has provided over many years."

David Packard,
Deputy Secretary of Defense

IF MANY Lockheed stockholders still felt their company had taken them for a ride, despite its "clean bill of health" from the SEC, they could take some comfort from the fact that the company had not enjoyed the trip either. As far back as September, 1968, the monthly cost reports Lockheed submitted to the Air Force began indicating that C–5A construction expenses were running so high the company might not make any profit on the program.[1] Up to that time, with the friendly cooperation of the Air Force, whenever costs had risen above target, Lockheed had simply revised the budget estimates upward. The Air Force had generally accepted the revisions and increased its payments correspondingly.

Early in 1969, before the first plane had been delivered, Lockheed asked the Air Force about the possibility of an "interim repricing formula adjustment" to help solve what it called "cash flow problems."[2] Translated, this simply meant that Lockheed was spending considerably more on the C–5A than it was receiving for the work from the Air Force, and wanted to invoke the contract's repricing formula at this point instead of after construction of the first 58 planes, as the contract called for. The Air Force did not agree to this proposal, but the fact that Lockheed even tried illustrates the degree to which many large defense contractors expect the Pentagon to watch out for them.

Not only did Lockheed have the use of largely government-owned plant and machinery, it also received weekly "progress payments" designed to cover most of its expenses on the C–5A. The Air Force took great care to see that Lockheed received this money immediately, with none of the processing delays that frequently occur in commercial transactions of such scope. Payments were made on the spot by the USAF disbursement office set up in Lockheed's Marietta plant.

For most defense contracts, progress payments normally run about 70 to 75 per cent of actual costs. The C–5A contract allowed for payments up to 90 per cent. When the General Accounting Office checked, however, it found that by the end of 1968 the Air Force had made C–5A progress payments to Lockheed amounting to $1.2 billion, against total costs of $1.278 billion — nearly 95 per cent.[3] In June, 1969, Lockheed submitted documents to the Senate Armed Services Committee disclosing that as of the end of May, on total costs of $1.569 billion, the company had received payments totaling $1.48 billion — also about 95 per cent. When he learned of this situation, Senator Harry Byrd pointed out that by using these funds supplied by the Defense Department, "Lockheed has gotten the advantage of somewhere around $150 million worth of interest, because the Government has to borrow this money . . . It seems to me that Lockheed has been operating entirely on Federal funds."[4]

Under DoD regulations, progress payments can cover "all costs which are reasonable, allocable to the contract, and consistent with sound and generally accepted accounting principles and procedures." Since companies use a wide range of different accounting procedures, this regulation means that "reasonable costs" depend to a great extent on how a company keeps its books.

Lockheed's method of reporting costs for progress payments included such "accrued liabilities" as unpaid material invoices and billings from subcontractors. When the GAO tried to determine the extent of such accrued liabilities, its investigators were told "such information is not readily available." [5] In other words, the government really had no way to check on where the progress payments were actually going. While they may have been used to pay for the C-5A, for all the government knew they may also have been diverted to cover the costs of Lockheed's commercial projects.

In addition to progress payments, Lockheed also had the benefit of special "milestone payments" for meeting various goals on design, development, and construction of the C-5A. Despite the fact that the program had already slipped by at least one year in its schedule, Lockheed had received many of these milestone payments. Combined with the progress payments, they occasionally brought Air Force payments to Lockheed up to 100 per cent of costs on the C-5A. When he learned about these bonus payments at a subcommittee hearing, Senator Proxmire exploded: "Special milestones! They are $2 billion over the original estimate, the most fantastic overrun I ever heard of, and they are getting special milestone achievement payments?" [6]

Despite the milestone payments, progress payments, "revised" budgets, and other forms of Pentagon generosity, Lockheed was running into increasingly serious trouble with the C-5A contract. During the Senate debate in September, 1969, when Proxmire urged a 90-day delay to allow time for a full-scale GAO investigation of the C-5A program, the Pentagon warned that any delay in government funding might cause Lockheed to default on its contract. Proxmire found this outrageous: "This kind of argument seems to me to come close to placing the Senate in the position of one who is being blackmailed. It sounds like someone is delivering an ultimatum: 'Pay up a half a billion dollars as an installment on the fourth squadron, or the Government does not get the first three squadrons.' . . . Is the Federal Government so intimidated by its contractors that it must continue to dole out public money for new contracts, regardless of whether or not they are needed, so that the contractors will not default on the old contracts? Do defense contractors have such a stranglehold on the Government that it is really they, not us, who control the public purse strings?" [7]

The answer to this question became clear during the following months. When the Pentagon finally decided to limit the C–5A program to 81 planes, or four squadrons, word leaked out that the Air Force had begun to renegotiate the C–5A contract to allow Lockheed to break even on the 81 planes, instead of the full 115 the company had planned on. This sounded as if the Air Force was offering to swallow what some officials had estimated as a potential loss of $675 million on the 81-plane order.

Even this did not seem to be enough. Early in 1970, rumors circulated on Capitol Hill that Lockheed was threatening to go into bankruptcy if the Air Force did not come up with massive financial relief for the C–5A program. When he heard these reports, Senator Proxmire wrote Assistant Air Force Secretary Philip Whittaker, urging the Air Force to "enforce the terms of the contract," and if not, to make its financial dealings with Lockheed public.[8]

One week later, on March 5, 1970, the Pentagon did just that, releasing what must certainly be one of the most extraordinary letters ever received by any government agency. On corporate stationery bearing the slogan "Look to Lockheed for Leadership," board chairman Daniel Haughton wrote Deputy Secretary of Defense David Packard that unless Lockheed received an additional $435 to $500 million to cover its expenses on the C–5A

program, the company would have to halt production. Haughton
explained that although the $600 million C–5A contract dispute
had gone to the Armed Services Board of Contract Appeals, the
board would not make a ruling on the case before late 1971. Even
then, its ruling might be appealed to the U.S. Court of Claims,
which could drag the case out until 1973, or 1974. Lockheed
simply could not wait that long. "The unprecedented dollar
magnitude of the differences to be resolved" wrote Haughton, "make it impossible for Lockheed to complete performance
[of the C–5A program] if we must await the outcome of litigation
before receiving further financing from the Department of Defense." Reminding Packard that the C–5A program was "essential
to the nation's defense," Haughton warned, "we cannot maintain
uninterrupted performance" without "significant financial assistance" from the Pentagon.[9] The choice he offered was perfectly
clear: Pay up, or lose the C–5A.

While Lockheed definitely had legal precedent for its request,
the biggest such "relief" package anyone could recall was a $55
million "provisional claim" granted to Todd Shipbuilding Corporation in 1969. Lockheed was asking for nearly ten times that
amount for the C–5A. In addition, the company's March letter
to the Pentagon listed claims totaling $335 million on three other
defense contracts: $175 million for a series of 9 ships, $110
million for the Cheyenne helicopter, and $50 million for the Short
Range Attack Missile (SRAM). To continue work on these
other programs, Lockheed wanted a total of $155 million in im-
mediate "interim financing." Lockheed blamed most of its troubles with these programs on their total package procurement contracts, but as *Fortune* magazine commented, "any company that
can lose huge sums of money on four defense contracts at the
same time must be doing *something* wrong." [10]

The response to Lockheed's request came quickly from Capitol

Hill. Otis Pike called for a speedy resolution of the C–5A contract dispute, but said, "to go beyond that, and just give the money, is a kind of defense blackmail we just can't yield to." Representative William Moorhead warned the Pentagon against "bailing out" Lockheed without seeking congressional approval. He compared the company's threat to that of "an 80-ton dinosaur who comes to your door and says, 'If you don't feed me, I will die. And what are you going to do with 80 tons of dead, stinking dinosaur in your yard?' "[11]

Representative George Mahon (Dem.-Tex.), the powerful chairman of the House Appropriations Committee, blamed Lockheed management for the company's troubles: "They just didn't do a good job on the C–5A. They made a lot of mistakes." Mahon did not want to "throw good money after bad," but he insisted "we have to have this aircraft . . . To wash this thing out with just a few planes would be a vast loss."[12] Mahon probably did not fully appreciate just how bad the loss would actually be. By July, 1970, with only nine defective planes delivered, the Air Force had paid Lockheed a total of $2.5 billion.

Senator Proxmire suggested that Lockheed was "attempting to develop a new way to pay for massive cost overruns" and charged that its request for financial aid was "only a variation of one of the oldest military procurement themes: buy-in-now, get-well-later." He asked the U.S. Comptroller General "to immediately undertake an investigation of the financial condition of Lockheed, and its ability to continue performance of its military contracts." He wrote Defense Secretary Laird to inform him of this GAO study and to ask that the Pentagon take no action on the Lockheed request until Congress had a chance to consider the GAO report.[13]

News of the extent of the financial crisis faced by Lockheed, the nation's largest defense contractor, sent shock waves through-

out the rest of the aerospace industry. Some firms reacted by putting greater energy into their efforts to shift away from near total
reliance on defense contracts. Other firms reacted the way any
normal children would react if they heard the neighborhood candy
store was about to pass out free candy. As one major West Coast
defense contractor put it, "My response was simple. I told my
people to go stand in line." Within two weeks of the announcement of Lockheed's request, the Air Force alone received more
than 400 letters from firms interested in similar financial assistance.[14]

Back in Burbank, California, officials at Lockheed headquarters
were lying low during this crucial period, careful not to say anything that might antagonize anyone at the Pentagon or on Capitol
Hill. Chairman Haughton, all sweetness and reason, said, "We
appreciate the prompt attention which Secretary Packard and the
Pentagon are giving to our requests. We are hopeful that an early
solution which is equitable to the interests of both the Government and the company can be reached." [15] Lockheed president
A. Carl Kotchian, trying to defuse what many had taken as a
threat, told reporters the company would certainly continue work
on the C–5A, "pending a reply" from the Pentagon. All the
company really expected, said Kotchian, was an assurance that
it would receive sufficient financial support to enable it to complete the contract. "We didn't go in there with a tin cup, asking
them to fill it up right away." [16] In a move designed to build up
public support for congressional action on its request, Lockheed
also tried to argue its case in the mass media. Departing from
its normal trade magazine advertising, the company ran two-page
C–5A ads in *Time* and *Newsweek*, hailing the plane's marvelous
capabilities, most of which had still not been successfully demonstrated.

Officially, the Pentagon announced the Lockheed request was
being given "priority consideration by the appropriate officials."

Privately, some of these officials expressed the general opinion that the Defense Department simply could not allow Lockheed to go under, regardless of the extent of its financial problems. As the sole source of the Polaris and Poseidon ICBM missiles, along with dozens of other major weapon systems, Lockheed's continued corporate health was more than simply a legal or financial question for the Pentagon.

Lockheed's financial condition worried the White House at least as much as it did the Pentagon. With November, 1970, congressional elections approaching, the Republican administration did not want the blame for the bankruptcy of a corporation that employed 100,000 men in 25 states. The government had been unable to save the Penn Central from financial collapse around this same time, but Lockheed was five times the size of Penn Central in terms of gross annual revenues. Its demise would have shaken the entire economy and would have represented a political catastrophe for the Nixon administration.

In seeking help for Lockheed, the Pentagon first turned to the banking community. On March 4, the day before he announced the Lockheed request, Packard and other top DoD officials met privately with six of the country's leading bankers to discuss the possibility of commercial loans. The bankers were understandably cool to Packard's plea, for only eight months before, Lockheed had arranged for a $400 million "line of credit" from a consortium of 24 banks. The purpose of that loan had been to finance Lockheed's commercial ventures, but because of mounting costs on the Galaxy, most of the money had been diverted to the C–5A program. By the time of its request to the Pentagon, Lockheed had drawn nearly $300 million against the line of credit, but still found itself desperately short of cash. "They're hocked to the hilt," said a rival industry executive. "They've already put the house, wife and dog up for sale." [17]

All of these problems made Lockheed an unattractive candidate for any further sizable loans. Because of its shaky financial state, any loans that could be arranged at this time would only have been extended at prohibitively high rates of interest. The bankers told Packard that Lockheed had only three real options: merger with another, healthier aerospace firm; bankruptcy and reorganization; or some kind of emergency loan backed up by the Pentagon itself. "After all," said one of the bankers later, in favor of the third approach, "Lockheed is an integral part of defense." [18]

Another option discussed at this meeting with the bankers was the possibility of a special stock issue to raise the needed funds. Lockheed's financial plight, however, would make such an offering as unattractive to investors as its loan application would be to banks. Lockheed stock had already fallen from a 1969–70 high of $50 a share to less than $16 on the day the Pentagon released the company's request for $500 million. The rest of the aerospace industry, and the stock market in general, had also declined during this period, but not as badly as Lockheed. At the time of its emergency request, $500 million represented nearly three times the total value of its outstanding stock. Later that same day, Lockheed announced a net loss for 1969 of $32.6 million, in contrast to 1968 profits of $44.5 million. The New York Stock Exchange had halted trading in Lockheed prior to the Pentagon's morning announcement of the aid request, and by the following day Lockheed stock had fallen below $15, its lowest price since 1960.

On the basis of Packard's March 4, 1970, meeting with the bankers, the Defense Department decided to go to Congress on Lockheed's behalf. The following week, Packard told the House Armed Services Committee that some form of public support — either a government loan, an outright grant, or an immediate negotiated settlement of the contract dispute — were the only "attractive solutions" to Lockheed's money problems. Packard recognized such other solutions as merger and reorganization, but apparently considered them unattractive. According to Packard, "there is no question about the need to preserve this important capability which Lockheed has provided over many years." Whatever the final solution, Packard promised the committee the Defense Department would take all necessary steps to protect "the Government's interest." Despite this expressed concern for the government's interest, Packard still seemed at least equally concerned for the welfare of Lockheed. Although he told the HASC that the "attractive" methods of solving Lockheed's problem required immediate congressional appropriation, he told reporters after the hearing that the Pentagon would somehow find the necessary funds to support Lockheed until Congress reached a decision. "We've been helping them out," said Packard, "and we'll continue to help them out until we get a final solution." [19]

By April, the GAO had turned its latest C–5A report over to Senator Proxmire, who not surprisingly found that it lacked the financial information on Lockheed he had requested. He then asked the Pentagon for a "cash flow" statement on Lockheed. DoD informed him that it did not have one available, but would prepare one in two weeks. Later the Pentagon changed its position and simply refused to provide a Lockheed cash flow statement on the grounds that it would involve "proprietary information." (Since by this time Lockheed was almost totally dependent on the government, it is hard to see how such information could any longer be considered proprietary.) Proxmire was shocked by the fact that the Pentagon did not already have a cash flow statement before requesting help from Congress. He described it as "the most fundamental information necessary for an analysis of short term cash needs . . . No bank in its right mind would extend substantial credit to a corporation without seeing a cash flow statement." Without one, he charged, "no one in the Congress or the Department of Defense has the facts on which to base an intelligent decision on the Lockheed request." He criticized the Pentagon for what he called "an appalling lack of knowledge about Lockheed's financial condition . . . It is inconceivable to me that a Government agency could have placed literally billions of dollars worth of military contracts with a corporation while knowing so little about the corporation and its ability to perform its contracts." [20]

Through various sources during the next few weeks, Proxmire did manage to learn enough about Lockheed's finances to make him even more skeptical about what he called the Pentagon's attempt to "bail the company out." According to certain high Pentagon officials, said Proxmire, Lockheed's current financial crisis was "triggered by difficulties on its commercial ventures with the L–1011 aircraft, and not by its government contracts." Because of a sharp decline in the commercial aviation industry, Lockheed had only received about 100 firm orders for its L–1011, a tri-jet airbus, not nearly enough to break even on its production. (Industry sources put Lockheed's break-even point on the L–1011 at 225 planes.) Proxmire charged that the company's troubles with the L–1011, combined with the enormous cost overrun on the C–5A, had brought it to "the brink of bankruptcy." [21] Lockheed immediately issued a denial of the senator's charges, calling them a "distortion," but did not offer any specific evidence to refute them. A company spokesman also denied the threat of bankruptcy, saying Lockheed hoped "such statements will be avoided in the future." [22]

The following week Senator Proxmire disclosed that the Palmdale, California, plant in which Lockheed was building its commercial L–1011 was a government-owned facility leased to Lockheed on generous terms by the Air Force. "It is bad enough," said Proxmire, "that the C–5A is being built in a government-owned plant, with government-owned machinery, and with government progress payments up to 90 per cent of the actual costs. Now we find that Lockheed's commercial ventures are being produced in a government-owned plant under a rental arrangement which gives every indication that it is a 'sweetheart contract.' " Proxmire charged that this arrangement "reinforces the appearance of a sustained effort on the part of the Air Force to assist the commercial activities of one of its major contractors." [23]

Of all the journalistic comments on the Lockheed crisis, the most serious criticism came from *Armed Forces Journal*, probably the most respected publication on military and defense industry affairs. In an editorial by publisher (and former Boeing executive) Benjamin Schemmer, the *Journal* called Packard's decision to seek congressional aid "precipitous." "We find it hard," wrote Schemmer, "to understand the haste with which Mr. Packard came to his conclusion." Schemmer pointed out that Packard himself told Congress that DoD had sufficient funds in its current budget to cover Lockheed's C–5A costs for the rest of 1970 — another eight months. "If DoD bails Lockheed out, without first asking a lot more questions than we've seen Mr. Packard discuss with Congress so far, we'll have learned little, but paid plenty." Schemmer questioned Packard's hasty dismissal of reorganization or merger as "unattractive" solutions to Lockheed's problem. "Why not reorganize or merge Lockheed?" he asked. "There's ample precedent: McDonnell-Douglas, North American-Rockwell, and Republic Aviation-Fairchild-Hiller, to name a few recent ones . . . Is Lockheed still the right company to manage the C–5A? If the program is as 'essential' as Mr. Packard says, why not put a new team into the Marietta plant to manage the program? If Lockheed can't manage, perhaps it needs new management who can." [24]

Publisher Schemmer was not the first to recommend such stiff measures in order to solve the kind of problem Lockheed found itself with. In testimony before a House subcommittee, Gordon Rule, the Navy's top civilian procurement official, argued, "If defense contractors can't hack it, they ought to be terminated for default. If they lose money, and go bankrupt, let them do it. Maybe a couple of bankruptcies and defaults in the industry [will] do them good." [25]

Even the threat of such drastic action had proved successful in the past. In 1964, the Defense Department became embroiled in a dispute with General Dynamics over production costs for the Standard Missile. When the company threatened to halt production unless its demands were met, the Pentagon hired Ernest Fitzgerald, then a private consultant, to investigate the program. Through informal inquiries Fitzgerald learned that several other firms would have been able and delighted to take over the management of the program. The only persons who would have been affected by such a change, he discovered, were about two dozen General Dynamics executives who would lose their jobs. Fitzgerald felt that since their management of the program had been the primary cause of its troubles, their departure would not have been a serious loss. Confronted with the prospect of a forced reorganization, General Dynamics suddenly decided it could complete the missile program after all. [26]

"This happens all the time," says Fitzgerald today. "When things are going well, the companies stress the idea of free enterprise, with no need for government regulation. But when things aren't going well, they suddenly become a 'close partner' with the government, and want it to bail them out. All they have to do is threaten to collapse, and the government pours in more money. In the past such bail-outs were handled routinely through contract change orders. What's unusual about this Lockheed situation is that it has become public." [27]

The talk of merger and reorganization, in addition to Proxmire's disclosures, the Bisplinghoff Report, and the criticism in
the press, did little to enhance Lockheed's position in the stock
market, nor to help Packard's plea for congressional aid. By the
time he appeared before the SASC late in May, 1970, Lockheed
stock had dropped from $16 in March to $9 a share. By then,
Packard's view of which solutions to Lockheed's problem were
attractive had changed. This time he felt "no resolution can be
achieved short of bankruptcy . . . without financial support
from the private sector." He said he had "urged" Lockheed officials to seek financial assistance through commercial loans, "and
even through merger, in order to preserve their capability." He
insisted that the Pentagon's goal was to preserve production of the
C–5A, not necessarily Lockheed itself. He went so far as to
imply that the Pentagon was prepared to take over production of
the plane itself if Lockheed balked at reorganization. (Taking
over Lockheed would hardly be as revolutionary as it might at first
sound. For several years, about 90 per cent of the company's
business had been with the government, mostly the Department of
Defense. Lockheed-Georgia did virtually all its work for DoD. In
fact, industry wits had been referring to Lockheed for some time
as a "wholly-owned subsidiary" of the Pentagon.)

Despite all the talk of multiple options and attractive solutions,
the plan Packard finally came up with to solve Lockheed's money
crisis did not differ a great deal from the manner in which the
Pentagon had customarily handled such problems in the past.
Packard asked Congress to authorize a special $200 million "con-
tingency fund" for the C–5A, in addition to the $344 million
already budgeted for it in the fiscal 1971 military procurement
bill. He promised the Pentagon would not spend the extra $200
million "until satisfactory contractual arrangements are concluded." If Congress failed to provide the extra money, Packard
warned, it "would in effect be curtailing the C–5A program." [28]

Something else occurred about this time which, had anyone done anything about it, might have also curtailed or reduced the C–5A program, with considerable savings for the public. At a special demonstration in Seattle for members of the House Military Airlift Subcommittee, Boeing unveiled a military cargo version of its 747. This 747C could handle nearly all the heavy equipment for which the C–5A had been designed since the 747 itself had grown out of Boeing's bid for the C–5A contract in 1965. It also had several additional virtues: its landing gear worked, its wings did not crack, and it would cost less than half the price of the C–5A. According to a Boeing proposal, the Pentagon could save $676 million by limiting its C–5A buy to 58 aircraft and supplementing them with 20 747Cs. By stopping the C–5A order at two squadrons, or 38 planes, and buying 32 of Boeing's 747Cs, the savings would amount to nearly a billion dollars.[29]

None of these figures seemed to have much effect on the Pentagon or Congress. Pentagon sources indicated that while DoD officials were "aware" of comparative cost studies on the two planes, no one had given any serious thought to cutting back further than 81 C–5As. When the Military Airlift Subcommittee returned to Washington, D.C., its chairman, Representative Melvin Price (Dem.-Ill.), announced that he could see "no alternative" to buying all four C–5A squadrons. In fact, Price later told a meeting of Washington's Aerospace Club, an industry group, that he thought the Defense Department should order two more C–5A squadrons from Lockheed to meet "future cargo needs." [30]

No one really expected any serious congressional opposition to what became known as Lockheed's $200 million "slush fund." After all, $200 million seemed like such a small sum compared to the cost of the total program. (It is also more than the U.S.

government spends on the entire federal judicial system.) Many congressmen simply felt that Lockheed had to be preserved. As HASC chairman Mendel Rivers put it, "This aerospace industry has some great people in it. We can't sit back and see them wiped out. Somebody has got to work for them." [31]

As long as Lockheed and the aerospace industry have men like Mendel Rivers working for them, they won't need many other friends on Capitol Hill. Rivers rammed the contingency fund through the HASC, over the objections of Otis Pike. Pike could not understand why Congress should authorize the payment of money to Lockheed that, according to DoD's claim in the C–5A contract dispute, it did not owe. "Here is a situation," Pike complained, "where the Air Force says 'We do not owe them money,' and the Secretary of Defense says, 'Yes, but we have to be ready to give it to them anyway.' " [32]

When Rivers appeared before the House Rules Committee in April to discuss the handling of the 1971 military procurement bill, he again argued that three hours would be sufficient time for debate. Rules Committee chairman Representative William Colmer (Dem.-Miss.) agreed. (Colmer was not particularly concerned about the C–5A, but he did ask Rivers to "consider" including a road in Colmer's district in the military construction bill. Rivers promised to study this request seriously.) [33] When the procurement bill reached the House floor in May, Otis Pike introduced an amendment to cut out the extra $200 million for Lockheed, but Rivers warned that if the amendment passed, "you can kiss your airlift goodbye." The House rejected the Pike amendment, 90 to 48. [34]

The Senate later defeated a similar amendment offered by Senator Schweiker, 48 to 30. However, in a move that indicated the C–5A affair was beginning to have some effect, the Senate version of the bill required the Pentagon to submit a plan to the

SASC before spending any of the $200 million fund. The Senate version also specifically prohibited the use of the money for any project other than the C-5A.

Air Force officials in Washington spent the summer of 1970 trying to devise a solution to the C-5A contract dispute that would be satisfactory to the Pentagon and Lockheed, if not to the public. On the strength of the $200 million contingency fund voted by Congress, Lockheed managed to raise the promise of another $150 million in credits from its bankers during that summer.[35] This new loan, however, would be dependent on a speedy settlement of Lockheed's contract dispute with the Defense Department. Always eager to oblige, the Air Force quickly came up with a plan that would circumvent the Armed Services Board of Contract Appeals — the government's legal channel for litigating such disputes.

In an August 31 briefing paper marked "For Official Use Only," the Air Force argued that Lockheed could not hold off bankruptcy until the ASBCA made its ruling in the case and that if the ruling went against Lockheed, the company would face a "catastrophic loss." [36] Instead of waiting, the Air Force proposed settling Lockheed's $600 million C-5A claim at a compromise figure of $200 to $300 million and providing the difference in the form of a long-term, low interest government loan. The repayment period under these liberal terms would only start in 1974 and could last up to 40 years. The Air Force suggested that the loan be made under Public Law 85-804, which enables the Pentagon to make loans unilaterally, with no assurance of the recipient's ability to repay, instead of the more commonly used Defense Production Act, which requires a Federal Reserve Board credit analysis of any company seeking a federally guaranteed loan. P.L. 85-804 provides for financial relief to companies deemed "essential to the national defense" and is valid only in time of "national emergency." But since no one has ever bothered to rescind the state of emergency declared by President Truman in 1950 during the Korean War, the law is still in effect. All the Pentagon has to do is declare that Lockheed's financial emergency represents a national emergency.

In addition to the compromise settlement and the long-term loan, the Air Force briefing paper suggested that a new C–5A contract be drawn up, allowing for payment of Lockheed's production costs without regard to the ceiling set by the existing contract. The proposed contract would set a maximum "fixed loss" for Lockheed based not upon the contract price, but upon the "ability of Lockheed to tolerate loss." Under the new contract the Air Force would drop the $11 million late delivery penalty, add up to $10 million as a "termination allowance," and throw in an extra $25 million as an "award fee" for superior performance.

During the fall and winter of 1970, under the threat of bankruptcy, Lockheed tried to negotiate a settlement of the C–5A dispute with the Pentagon. Finally, on February 1, 1971, Lockheed "reluctantly" agreed to a Pentagon proposal under which the government would pay $758 million in disputed production costs, in exchange for which the company would drop its legal claims and accept a fixed loss of $200 million, to be paid back over a ten-year period. This tentative settlement collapsed three days later, however, upon the bankruptcy of Britain's Rolls-Royce Ltd., which was to make the engines for Lockheed's commercial L–1011 airbus. The demise of Rolls-Royce not only shook the British empire, it left Lockheed without engines for its L–1011. With the future of its airbus in doubt, Lockheed again faced the specter of bankruptcy.

CHAPTER FIFTEEN

What Everyone Learned
from the C-5A

*"I don't see why everyone has picked on the C-5A.
There are many examples of defense contracting that
are much worse."*

Robert Anthony,
Assistant Secretary of Defense
(Comptroller), 1965–1968

AT LOCKHEED'S ANNUAL MEETING in May, 1970, board chairman Daniel Haughton told stockholders assembled out at the
Burbank, California, headquarters that although the C-5A contract dispute was still unsettled, he felt confident the company's
problems would be solved "one way or another." [1]

Mr. Haughton is undoubtedly right. One way or another the
Air Force will get its planes and Lockheed will be paid. One
way or another Congress will authorize the necessary funds and
the taxpayers of America will have to come up with the money.
But after an enterprise as costly and controversial as the C-5A
affair, one would expect that, in addition to merely settling their
mutual problems and disputes, the various parties involved would
have learned something of value from the experience — something that might help them avoid similar misfortunes with future
defense programs. One would hope their reactions to the C-5A
affair would show that, at least in this way, the program had been
profitable.

Certainly Lockheed had good reason to reflect upon its experience with the C-5A. Estimates of the company's potential loss on
the program, depending on the outcome of its contract dispute

with the Air Force, run as high as $600 million — enough to wipe the company out of business. Many of Lockheed's subcontractors have equal reason to be disillusioned with the C–5A and feel that Lockheed is to blame. Conductron Corporation (a subsidiary of McDonnell Douglas), which built the C–5A flight simulators, is pressing claims of $20 million against Lockheed for contract adjustments. Kaman Corporation, which produced the plane's wing surfaces, has sued Lockheed for $18 million, on the grounds that Lockheed changed designs in midproduction, unfairly running up Kaman's costs.[2] If Kaman wins its suit, other C–5A subcontractors may also sue Lockheed.

If its subcontractors blamed Lockheed for their troubles with the C–5A, Lockheed in turn blamed the Pentagon. More specifically, and in order not to unduly antagonize its primary source of income, it blamed the Total Package Procurement Concept upon which the C–5A contract had been based. In his March letter asking for financial aid, Haughton wrote that "without disregarding our own deficiencies," most of the company's problems with the C–5A had resulted from the restrictions and inadequacies of a contract that had proved to be "virtually unworkable."[3] In addition to the contract, Haughton felt the critics in the press and Congress had also been partly responsible for his company's troubles. He claimed they had unfairly exaggerated the C–5A's cost and technical problems. The aerospace industry, he complained, faces "a hostile environment in which some people abuse anyone or any company that is working to defend his country."[4]

And what of the Pentagon? Like any totalitarian regime with a well-publicized failure on its hands, the Pentagon reacted by striking out at its critics, both internal and external. Internally this meant a purge of dissident elements. The beauty of a purge at such times is that it diverts attention from the real, embarrassing problem and gives an impression of corrective action. It also provides a useful excuse to dismantle offices or dismiss people who may have been troublesome anyway by implying their responsibility for whatever went wrong.

In the case of the C-5A scandal, the first victim had to be Ernest Fitzgerald, the man who first brought the $2 billion cost overrun to the public's attention. The Pentagon not only got rid of Fitzgerald, it abolished his job, making sure that no successor would make similarly embarrassing revelations. This showed the Pentagon's intention of purging not those responsible for the C-5A's problems, but those whose criticism and opposition had made them a public affair. Instead of trying to cure its disease, the patient fired the doctor.

Next the Defense Department went to work on its civilian Office of Systems Analysis. Charged with keeping a check on the cost effectiveness of major weapon systems, OSA had had the poor judgment to produce a study questioning the need for six C-5A squadrons. Since OSA had been questioning the need for many of the services' pet projects, the services began openly questioning the need for OSA. With the energetic support of Mendel Rivers, they urged Secretary Laird to simply abolish OSA, as he had done with Fitzgerald's job.

A move of such magnitude, however, required a bit more finesse. First the Pentagon announced that much of the work previously done by civilians at OSA would be transferred to the separate services, where it would be supervised by "proper military authority." [5] In other words, the generals would be in charge of checking their own judgment. Then the five OSA posts previously included in the Pentagon's list of "executive level positions" were quietly dropped from that list. As for Dr. Ivan Selin, the acting Assistant Secretary of Defense for OSA, Secretary Laird just didn't get around to submitting his name to the Senate for confirmation. Most of the men at OSA quickly took the hint and left the Defense Department for more appreciative employers.[6]

The first opportunity to observe the new atmosphere at the Pentagon came with the award of a contract to McDonnell Douglas for the F–15, a new Air Force jet fighter. This was the first major contract negotiated and signed by the Laird regime, and there was much talk about "tough" new contracting methods. The Pentagon announced proudly that this time there would be no chance for any civilians in the Office of the Secretary of Defense "to monitor or interfere" with the Air Force's management of the program.[7]

As time passed, the results of this "new" management method seemed strikingly familiar to those who had followed the progress of the C–5A. In June, 1969, the Pentagon told Congress it planned to buy about 500 F–15s, at an average cost of $5 to $7 million apiece, "excluding spares, etc." In September, Air Force Secretary Seamans said he was "shooting for" a unit cost of $6 to $8 million. When the Pentagon announced the award to Mc-Donnell Douglas, in December, 1969, General Benjamin Bellis, director of the F–15 program, told reporters he expected to eventually buy 700 planes at an average price of $13.5 million — for a total cost of nearly $10 billion. Secretary Seamans promised that this time the Air Force would control costs on the program by requiring "good, hard estimates." [8]

Having thus solved its internal problems, the Pentagon had to do something about the unpleasant publicity caused by the C–5A. Again the solution involved fixing the blame on a handy scapegoat. As much as some officials would have liked to, however, the Air Force was unable to discover anyone responsible for the C–5A fiasco. Upon his retirement, USAF Chief of Staff General McConnell seemed particularly concerned about this problem. "In running flying squadrons, I never had any trouble," he told the Senate Defense Appropriations Subcommittee. "When a squadron commander goofed, he was fired. In our procurement and development areas, I can't find anyone to fire. Too many people at too many levels have had too much to say about the program." [9]

Since policies are more expendable and defenseless than people, the Pentagon gradually settled — as had Lockheed — upon the Total Package Procurement concept as the villain in the C–5A affair. In fact, the contract turned out to be the perfect villain. It was the creation of the previous Democratic regime and was closely associated with the arch-villain McNamara. Its actual creator, Robert Charles, had already left, so no one currently at the Pentagon had to feel any responsibility for it. Appearing before the HASC, which only two years before had heard Mc-Namara praise the Total Package Procurement method, Deputy Secretary Packard called it "a very inadequate instrument." To improve DoD's contracting procedures, Packard issued a new policy directive in June, 1970, placing greater stress on the conceptual and development stages on new weapon systems and allowing for "greater flexibility" in the negotiation of ultimate prices and requirements.[10]

In another policy directive, Packard tackled the problem of cost overruns in a manner befitting the legendary emperor who found himself without clothes. In a memorandum to senior DoD officials, Packard urged that the term "cost overrun" be dropped from the Pentagon's vocabulary because of its "imprecise meaning." (Somehow, Packard's memo did not circulate fast enough or high enough to prevent Secretary Laird from using the term "cost overrun" twice that same day, during testimony before the Senate Appropriations Committee.) The phrase "cost overrun," wrote Packard in his memo, created "confusion in the minds of many" and cast an "improper reflection on the true status of events." He recommended using "cost growth" instead.[11] Whether "cost growth" will create any less confusion or cast more proper reflections than "cost overrun" is debatable, although "growth" does have a certain positive sound to it.

To make sure that only the "true status" of the C–5A reached the public, Packard classified virtually all information on the program. Queries on the C–5A from reporters and even congressional staff aides ran into a wall of censorship. The Air Force even refused to help one House legislative aide who simply called to ask how many planes there were in a squadron. An Air Force public information officer told him Packard had classified the C–5A as a "sensitive program." [12] Information on it could only be released upon written request, and even then only after being "coordinated" through Packard's office.

With most of these measures, the Pentagon was obviously trying to cut down on public criticism of the C–5A program by withholding information from its critics. At a time of federal spending cuts, headlines about the C–5A's $2 billion cost overrun certainly would not help the Pentagon get its $70 billion fiscal 1971 budget through Congress.[13] To counteract the impression that his department was wasting billions of dollars, Laird described his $20 billion military procurement bill as "rock bottom" and "bare boned," claiming "It does not give room for Congressional cutting." General Earle Wheeler, then Chairman of the Joint Chiefs of Staff, warned Congress that the DoD weapons requests were near "the borderline of acceptable military risk."

In an effort designed to give "more comprehensive communication to Congress on defense issues," the three services beefed up their Offices of Legislative Liaison on Capitol Hill, working overtime to make sure that wavering congressmen appreciated the military — and political — risks involved in voting to cut the Defense budget. One Hill aide reported "the most concentrated effort to avoid Congressional cuts we have ever seen." A service official predicted, "We think Mr. Laird will get most of what he asks for." He did. In a year when many domestic programs and even NASA had their funds sharply reduced, the 1971 Defense budget survived in rather good shape. The Senate found enough fat in Laird's "rock-bottom" weapons budget to trim off $1.3 billion. In May, 1970, the House, guided by Mendel Rivers, cut just $34 million, less than one tenth of one per cent.

In August, a grateful aerospace industry showed its appecia-tion for Rivers' friendship and protection with a testimonial luncheon given by the Washington chapter of the Air Force Asso-ciation. Among the association's corporate sponsors for the luncheon were most of the country's major defense contractors, including Lockheed. Nearly 1200 industry executives, congress-men, Pentagon officials, generals, and admirals gathered in the Washington Hilton's International Ballroom to watch Rivers re-ceive the AFA's annual Distinguished American Award for "the preservation of those outstanding traditions and values of the United States." An Air Force ceremonial band played Sousa marches before lunch; an Air Force dance band — "the Airmen of Note" — played a pops concert during lunch; and after lunch the Army's Old Guard Fife and Drum Corps performed in their Revolutionary War uniforms. Major General Roy Terry, the Air Force chief of chaplains, gave the invocation, citing Rivers as an example for all Americans. Vice President Spiro Agnew praised his willingness to "go to bat for the so-called and often discredited military-industrial complex." Senator Strom Thurmond described Rivers as "a beacon of light in these troubled times" and claimed: "No man in America, including the President, has done more for national defense than has L. Mendel Rivers."

In December, 1970, at the age of 65, Mendel Rivers died, in Birmingham, Alabama. Despite his years of dominance over House military affairs, his departure is unlikely to result in any major shift in the behavior of the House Armed Services Com-mittee. His successor is another southern Democrat, 69-year-old Representative F. Edward Hébert, of Louisiana. A close friend of Rivers, Hébert shares his predecessor's respect for the Pentagon. As he told reporters at a recent press conference: "When I have a legal problem I go to a lawyer. When I have a bellyache I go to a doctor. And I go to the military for military problems." [14]

Though unhappy at the loss of Rivers the defense industry hailed Hébert's ascendancy in its trade journals with ill-concealed joy. They took special note when he announced: "The military industrial complex is a part of us — a necessary part . . . We need these people, and have to keep them alive." [15]

To Representative Otis Pike, neither the change from Rivers to Hébert, nor Hébert's sympathy for the military-industrial complex, seems likely to have much effect on the way Congress handles the Defense budget. He is convinced that "The great evil is not the military-industrial complex, but secrecy. Nobody — including Congress — knows what's going on. It's all classified . . . The military have no difficulty leaking classified documents to Congress and the press to support their views, but people who are opposed to them simply can't get their hands on anything." [16]

Things are no better over at the Senate Armed Services Committee. Stuart Symington, one of its ranking Democratic members, complains, "Getting information for this committee is like trying to dig something out of a hole." [17] Even committee chairman Stennis recently grumbled to Secretary Laird, "Now when you send people up here before us to testify about these programs, we want all the facts. We don't want to have to dig out these facts. These people should volunteer these facts. All too often they just plain don't give us the facts." Asked how the SASC reaches its decisions in the absence of facts, Stennis explained: "You have to take a lot on faith." [18]

If the Armed Services Committees function this way, one can imagine how much faith the other 80 senators and 400 representatives need when voting on military matters. The HASC, says Representative John Brademas (Dem.-Ind.), "reports out a bill typically on a Thursday and calls for a vote the following Monday or Tuesday. Since none of the rest of us really have time to study the issue, and because we want to do nothing out of ignorance which may jeopardize a strong national defense, in effect, what a majority of a subcommittee decides determines the view of the entire House." Brademas feels the committees themselves don't give the military budgets a critical examination. "Defense takes care of its emissaries on the Hill very well," he says. "The Defense Committees tend not to ask questions." The result? "Congress has allowed itself to be shunted aside." [19]

According to Representative William Moorhead, one reason the Armed Services Committees fail to ask the right questions is that they are sadly understaffed. Compared to the thousands of men over at the Pentagon who prepare the Defense budgets, the Armed Services Committees each have less than a dozen men on their professional staff. "When the military budget totaling over $80 billion comes before the Congress for authorization and appropriation," says Moorhead, "it can readily be seen that Congress is almost hopelessly handicapped in obtaining a thoroughgoing, independent analysis of the Pentagon's proposals." Besides, he adds, "When a military program is reported, it is shrouded in secrecy and complexity, and wrapped in the flag, so that any questioning of it is considered close to being unpatriotic." [20]

A good illustration of this reaction to dissent occurred during the Senate debate on the fiscal 1971 Defense budget. When Senator Proxmire and other critics of military spending tried to cut the C-5A and other programs, they were accused of trying to "disarm" the country and "playing into the hands of the enemy." An editorial in *Barron's,* the financial weekly, lumped them together with "all those who seek to dismantle U.S. defense" and noted that Proxmire's attacks on the military-industrial complex "have won plaudits for him in the *Communist Daily World*." [21] In a speech on the Senate floor, Senator Barry Goldwater charged that "left wing political elements" were engaged in "an organized effort to downgrade and weaken the defense posture of this nation." [22]

Those who have followed the C–5A story must have observed that in addition to secrecy, understaffing, and misguided patriotism, good, old-fashioned politics also plays a major role in determining congressional action on military legislation. Would the Senate Appropriations Committee have so readily come up with money for the C–5A in 1965 if it were not being built in Georgia, home of committee chairman Richard Russell? Did the fact that Lockheed built a plant in Charleston, or that the first C–5A squadron went to Charleston AFB have any influence on the HASC, headed by Charleston's own Mendel Rivers? Were some congressmen from the 40 other states in which 2000 subcontractors worked on the C–5A program any less critical of the plane than they would otherwise have been? Senator William Fulbright thinks so: "I've had Congressmen tell me they wanted to vote against some of these military bills, but they just couldn't do it, because it would hurt the economy of their states." [23]

If this seems a bit crass to the layman, most congressmen quickly learn that voting against military programs which would bring contracts or bases to their districts is a good way to cut short a political career. Even those who oppose such crude politics usually succumb sooner or later. In a remarkably candid speech in 1959, Representative Ken Hechler (Dem.-W. Va.) told the House: "I am firmly against the kind of logrolling which would subject our defense program to narrowly sectional or selfish pulling or hauling. But I am growing pretty hot under the collar about the way my state of West Virginia is being short-

changed by the Army, Navy and Air Force." [24] Always interested
in stray votes on Capitol Hill, the Pentagon took the hint. Annual
defense contracts in West Virginia rose from $36 million at the
time of Hechler's speech to nearly $150 million in 1969.

Any congressman so selfless, unpatriotic, ignorant, or suicidal
as to oppose a military program will certainly be approached by
the Pentagon's $4 million, 370-man lobby on Capitol Hill. If
they fail to convince the errant legislator of the military value of
the program in question, they can often remind him of the economic benefits it will bring to his own state or district. In exchange for his support on crucial military programs, the Pentagon's
lobbyists can arrange various forms of gratitude: special leaves
or reassignments for the servicemen-sons of the congressman's
constituents; jobs for his supporters at military bases in his district; hunting trips on military reservations; free flights to and from
Washington on military planes; and "inspection trips" to such
trouble spots as Paris, Puerto Rico, and Hawaii.

The Air Force lobby on Capitol Hill dwarfs that of any other
federal agency or of any private industry or organization. The
USAF Office of Legislative Liaison has 177 men — more than
the combined legislative liaison staffs of the Departments of State,
HEW, Justice, Interior, Housing, Labor, Transportation, Agri-
culture, and Commerce. As effective advocates for defense programs, they serve the defense industry at least as much as the Air
Force. (In fact many of them become Washington representatives for the major defense contractors upon their retirement.)
The defense industry recognizes their value and leaves most of the
hard sell to them. As one member of the House Armed Services
Committee puts it: "The industry doesn't do much lobbying here
on the Hill. To sell a project to Congress is the hard way to do
it. It's much easier to sell the idea to the Air Force, and let the
Air Force do the pushing." [25] What all this means in terms of the

C-5A is that the public has not only paid an outrageous price for a defective plane, but has also paid the Air Force to convince the public's elected representatives to go along on the deal.

If the public interest occasionally suffers under such a system, it would hardly be an abnormal event on Capitol Hill. Anyone who sat through the Armed Services Committee hearings on the C-5A might easily conclude that Congress has little concern for the financial welfare of those who elected them. Congressmen and Air Force officials tossed the public's money about with carefree abandon: "a few hundred million . . . upward of a billion dollars, probably on the order of a billion and a half . . . of course, that's only a ballpark figure." As Representative Samuel Stratton observed during the HASC hearings on the C-5A, "We have been kicking billions around here so frequently that when there comes a difference of a few million you tend to neglect it." [26] Men dealing with their own money would probably demand a bit more precision in such discussions. But with the nation's security supposedly at stake, military procurement has never been a matter for rigorous accounting. As Senator Richard Russell once observed, "There is something about preparing for destruction that causes men to be more careless in spending money than they would be if they were building for constructive purposes." [27]

As for the generals, admirals, and Pentagon procurement officials, perhaps it is unreasonable to expect them to show any more respect for the public's money than a child would show for the allowance received from an overly generous father. The generals, however, play with bigger and more expensive toys. Former Defense Secretary McNamara once explained the psychology of military procurement in this fashion: "The military think about weapons the way women think about perfume." His point was that when a woman simply "must" have a certain perfume, price becomes irrelevant.

For this reason, when the estimated cost of each C-5A doubled from $20 million to $40 million, few people around the Pentagon seemed particularly upset. During the congressional hearings in June, 1969, when even the Pentagon was admitting a cost overrun on the C-5A of nearly 70 per cent, most Air Force officials felt this was "not a bad record" compared to other major Defense programs. Even former DoD Comptroller Robert Anthony (now back teaching accounting at Harvard Business School), who criticized the Air Force for its financial control of the C-5A program, says, "I don't see why everyone has picked on the C-5A. There are many examples of defense contracting that are much worse." [28]

Unfortunately Anthony is correct. Both in terms of percentage and actual dollars, the $2 billion C-5A cost overrun set no records in defense contracting. The Pentagon has already confirmed an overrun on the Minuteman II missile program of nearly $4 billion. Lockheed's Deep Submersible Rescue Vehicle, originally contracted by the Navy at $36.5 million for 12 models, is now estimated at $480 million for only 6 of them. This means the price of each DSRV has risen from $3 million to $80 million — a 2666 per cent cost increase. These are by no means exceptions. A recent General Accounting Office study of 38 major weapon programs currently underway showed an *average* cost rise already of 50 per cent over the original contract prices — and a total increase of $20 billion.[29]

A reasonable man confronted with these figures should begin to suspect that contract prices have little relation to actual costs, a fact which most Pentagon officials seem to take for granted. One man who doesn't is Gordon Rule, the Navy's top civilian contract official. At a hearing of Senator Proxmire's Subcommittee on Economy in Government, he gave this insider's complaint about the problem:

I think that one of the things that we have got to stop doing in our contracting is playing games — the government and the contractor. We play games. The contractors know that if they tell the Department of Defense how much something is really going to cost, DoD may scrub it. The Department of Defense knows if they tell the Congress the real cost, the Congress may scrub it. So you start in with both sides knowing that it is going to cost more. . . . This is what we do, and this is ridiculous. This is why we get into trouble.[30]

In a memo written about that time, Rule gave a detailed diagnosis of this trouble:

To me, the most important problem area is the inability of industry in this country to produce a quality product, on time, and at a reasonable cost — all three elements that are covered in the contracts which industry signs.

What is clearly needed is some tough-minded talk and action by representatives of the Government, who today are condoning and acquiescing in the failure of industry to perform as they should. . . . Industry today is smug, and perhaps rightly so. They know that no one in DoD is going to take any action they do not like, and today they have much justification for this attitude. No matter how poor the quality, how late the product, and how high the cost, they know nothing will happen to them. Until or unless this climate is changed, there will be little or no improvement in our procurements.[31]

Perhaps the person who learned most from the C–5A affair is Ernest Fitzgerald, and he is no longer in a position to do much about it. "The lesson I learned here," he told reporters who watched him clean out his desk at the Pentagon, "is that the bureaucracy is simply unwilling to hold a contractor to his commitments."[32] Fitzgerald sees this as a problem of attitude, rather than regulations. "In the three years and nine months I have worked in the Pentagon I have never heard a program manager propose cost reduction as a solution to a 'funding problem.' Cost reduction is simply not a recognized alternative when a weapons acquisition program starts running out of control." [33]

With such attitudes among those supposedly responsible for cost control, the usual approach to technical problems or rising costs is simply to conceal them by contract changes when possible, and by outright lying when necessary. According to Fitzgerald, "people don't realize how often the Pentagon lies about procurement costs. When a program goes bad, the military just plain lies about it. For example, we knew the C–5A was sick back in 1966, but no one would do anything about it. The worse it got the more they lied. My only fault was to commit truth.

"There won't be any more overruns in the Defense Department now, though. Everything will be classified, and there just won't be any records to base anything on. If you don't have records, you can't have overruns." [34]

One reason the Pentagon and the defense contractors continue to play such games is that, despite all the criticism of the military-industrial complex, the public still has almost no control over defense spending. The administration in power has shown no serious interest in cutting defense procurement costs, and except for a few brave souls, Congress does not seem to care about the problem, or does not recognize that a problem exists. The General Accounting Office, Congress's supposed "watchdog" on federal spending, has only recently begun devoting as much attention to the Defense budget as it has to the relatively minuscule federal poverty program. The press, except for occasional leaks, has access only to such information as the Pentagon chooses to release, none of it likely to be embarrassing.

To ensure that the public appreciates the military point of view, and to drum up support for each new weapon, the Pentagon propaganda machine will spend a total of nearly $40 million in 1971 through the Public Affairs Offices of each service and DoD.

Thus freed from any effective public criticism, the military establishment is free to conduct business as usual, a friendly partnership with the defense industry, with little concern for the public interest. From top to bottom, the military procurement system has a built-in bias favoring the industry point of view. Industry executives on DoD advisory commissions "help" set procurement policy. Top DoD officials are customarily drawn from the executive ranks of the defense industry, spend a few years at the Pentagon, and then return to the industry laden with inside knowledge and contacts.

When Melvin Laird chose David Packard as his Deputy Secretary of Defense, no one around the Pentagon worried about the fact that Packard had been a director of General Dynamics, or that his own company, Hewlett-Packard, had done — and still does — about a third of its business on defense contracts. No one seemed to mind that Robert Charles, the Air Force's top procurement official during most of the C–5A affair, had come from McDonnell Aircraft and then returned to Textron, another major defense firm. No one seemed to wonder about the objectivity of the 230 Air Force personnel assigned to Lockheed-Georgia as plant representatives supervising the C–5A's construction, even though some of them probably planned to join Lockheed upon their retirement. Such an expectation would hardly be unreasonable, since Lockheed already employs at least 200 retired generals, colonels, admirals, and Navy captains — more than any other defense contractor.

Because of such friendly relations, the $2 billion C–5A cost overrun gradually became a subject of humor in military-industrial circles. One current line used to calm anyone upset at cost increases of only a few million dollars runs: "Don't worry. They

waste that much in spilled coffee every day on the C–5A." At
the 1970 annual banquet of a military society called the Order
of the Carbao, an audience including Mendel Rivers and John
Stennis heard this musical tribute to the C–5A, sung to the tune
of "Wunderbar":

> C–5A, C–5A, history's biggest overrun,
> Raise the tax, and they'll pay
> For our costly C–5A.[35]

This carefree attitude toward spending the public's money is
typical of the manner in which the Air Force treated Lockheed
throughout the C–5A affair. It raises certain questions about the
nature of "free" or "private" enterprise in the defense industry.
On what grounds can a supposedly private firm like Lockheed
demand that the government absorb its losses on a contract merely
because it cannot complete the contract without the extra money?
To what extent is a company like Lockheed still "private" if 90
per cent of its business consists of government contracts, using
government-owned plants, government-owned machinery, and
government-supplied capital in the form of progress payments?
To what extent is the defense industry "free" enterprise if companies can tie themselves into huge contracts, without the threat
of competition, despite shoddy performance and gross mismanagement? In a speech during the C–5A debate in September,
1969, Senator William Fulbright described the defense industry
as "a degenerated form of socialism. Certainly there is no free
enterprise in it. There is no competition in it, and no efficiency
. . . It certainly is a distortion of what we are pleased to call a
private enterprise economic system." [36]

Distorted or not, the military-industrial complex marches on.
Air Force and Army generals are already talking about buying
an additional few squadrons of C–5As, partly because they want

them and partly to help out Lockheed. Meanwhile, Pentagon research men are already working on plans for a much bigger cargo aircraft, designated the LGX Megaplane. The proposed LGX would have a nuclear propulsion system and would carry 50 per cent more cargo than the giant C–5A. According to *Air Force* magazine, the LGX would meet "the increased airlift requirements of the more distant future." No one has come up with a cost estimate yet for the LGX, but the guessing starts at $100 million apiece. Even the LGX does not satisfy everyone, however. As an Air Force officer told reporters at the rollout of the first C–5A when they asked if it represented the ultimate plane, "Just as there is no ultimate weapon, there is no maximum plane." Perhaps not, in terms of technology, but at some point the cost of such technology becomes so ridiculous that only a madman would try to justify its necessity.

Anyone who has read this book should realize by now that the only remarkable aspect of the C–5A affair is that it became public, thanks to men like Fitzgerald, Proxmire, Moorhead, and Pike. Otherwise, the C–5A program was not particularly unusual. Its troubles had little to do with the plane itself. Rather, they are the natural result of the military-industrial-congressional system that produced it. Unfortunately, most of what happened to the C–5A happens to all military procurement programs. C–5As will continue to happen unless the public demands a change in the system. Until then, the public will have no choice but to continue paying the bills.

Research Documents on the C–5A
Notes
Index

Research Documents on the C–5A

THE FOLLOWING DOCUMENTS are necessary reading for any serious study of the C–5A affair. Some, like *The Congressional Record* and the congressional committee hearings, are readily available to the public in large libraries. Others, including the reports issued by the Air Force or the SEC, are not only unavailable to the general public, but extremely difficult to obtain even from the agencies which issued them. Anyone who has read this book should understand why. Documents cited frequently in these notes are referred to in the abbreviated form indicated below.

Joint Economic Subcommittee on Economy in Government (JEC) . . . Hearings on *Economics of Military Procurement* Part 1, November, 1968, and January, 1969

Hearings on *The Military Budget and National Economic Priorities* Parts 1 and 2, June, 1969

Hearings on *The Dismissal of A. Ernest Fitzgerald* November, 1969

House Government Operations Subcommittee on Military Operations (Mil Ops) . . . Hearings on *Government Procurement and Contracting* Part 4, April, 1969, pp. 1176–1227

House Armed Services Committee (HASC) . . . Hearings on *Military Procurement for Fiscal Year 1970* Parts 1 and 2, March–June, 1969

Senate Armed Services Committee (SASC) . . . Hearings on *Military Procurement for Fiscal Year 1970* Part 2, May–June, 1969, pp. 1993–2193

The Congressional Record, September–December, 1969

The Whitaker Report: *USAF Review of the C–5A Program*, July, 1969

The Bisplinghoff Report: *Report of the Ad Hoc Committee of the Air Force Scientific Advisory Board on the C–5A*, June, 1970

U.S. Securities and Exchange Commission (SEC) . . . *Report of Investigation in Re Lockheed Aircraft Corporation* HO–423, issued May 25, 1970, in two volumes

Harvard Business School case study on "Lockheed Georgia Company" Industrial Marketing #255, 1969

Lockheed Aircraft Corporation, Annual Reports, 1965–1969

The New York Times (Times), 1965–1970

The Washington Post (Post), 1965–1970

The Wall Street Journal (WSJ), 1965–1970

Armed Forces Journal (AFJ), 1965–1970

Air Force magazine (*Air Force*), 1965–1970

Notes

CHAPTER 1, The Birth of the Galaxy

1. For a discussion of the strategic concepts involved in the origin of the C–5A, see *Militarism U.S.A.* (New York: Scribner, 1970), by Colonel J. A. Donovan.
2. JEC, June, 1969, Part 1, p. 116.
3. *Fortune,* February, 1965, p. 52.
4. An official Air Force account of the selection process for the award of the C–5A contract can be found in SASC Part 2, June 3, 1969, pp. 2007–2028.
5. *Baltimore News American,* May 7, 1969.
6. Ibid.
7. *Times,* March 3, 1968.
8. *I. F. Stone's Weekly,* September 8, 1969.
9. SASC, pp. 2009–2010.
10. Ibid.

CHAPTER 2, The Contract and Mr. Charles

1. Robert Charles' speech, February 18, 1966, published by Harvard Business School, MM62.
2. *Baltimore News American,* February 9, 1969.
3. HASC Part 2, p. 3072.

4. Mil Ops, Part 5, p. 1426.
5. Charles' speech, op. cit.
6. *Fortune,* August, 1969. This article also contains a relatively clear analysis of the Total Package Procurement concept.
7. JEC, January, 1969, p. 321.
8. HASC, p. 3092.
9. SEC Report, Vol. I, p. 10.
10. Ibid., p. 12.
11. HASC, p. 3106.

CHAPTER 3, Construction, Confusion, and Concealment

1. SEC Report, Vol. I, p. 43.
2. Ibid., p. 17.
3. HASC, p. 2981.
4. Ibid.
5. HASC, p. 2981–2982.
6. HASC, p. 2986.
7. Ibid.
8. HASC, p. 2988–2989.
9. *The New Republic,* August 1, 1970, p. 21.
10. HASC, p. 2990.
11. HASC, p. 2944.
12. SEC Report, Vol. I, p. 32.
13. Ibid., p. 33.
14. Ibid., p. 34.
15. The report on the McConnell and Anthony memos can be found in *Post,* May 13, 1969.
16. Interview with author.
17. SEC Report, Vol. I, pp. 44–45.
18. Ibid., p. 46.
19. Mil Ops, Part 4, pp. 1177–1178.
20. *WSJ,* November 25, 1968.
21. Fitzgerald's account of his difficulties in getting cost information on the C–5A appears in JEC, January, 1969, pp. 336–337.
22. Mil Ops, Part 4, pp. 1221–1222.

23. HASC, pp. 3072–3073.
24. *Times,* March 3, 1969.
25. The Estes and Ferguson quotes and a description of the roll-out ceremony can be found in *Air Force,* April, 1968, p. 64.
26. *Newsweek,* March 11, 1968, p. 74.
27. The Sullivan quote and description of the first C–5A flight can be found in *Air Force,* October, 1968, p. 54.

CHAPTER 4, Options

1. Mil Ops, p. 1181.
2. JEC, November, 1968, pp. 199–210.
3. For an account of the GAO's difficulties, see JEC, January, 1969, pp. 254, 260–266, 321.
4. JEC, January, 1969, pp. 268–270.
5. *Business Week,* October 9, 1965.
6. *AFJ,* January 25, 1969.
7. For an analysis of this contract revision, see the *Washington Post,* August 20, 1970.
8. *Times,* January 17, 1969.
9. SASC, p. 2078.
10. SASC, p. 2184.
11. SASC, p. 2162.
12. *Post,* August 31, 1969.
13. JEC, January, 1969, p. 320.
14. For a concise comparison of the C–5A and 747, see *AFJ,* June 14, 1969.
15. HASC, pp. 3093–3095.
16. JEC, January, 1969, p. 316.
17. Ibid., p. 311.

CHAPTER 5, Committees

1. JEC, November, 1968, pp. 124–125.
2. *Air Force,* March, 1970, p. 38.
3. The story of Holifield's dispute with the GAO over missile costs

appears in *The Case Against Congress,* by Drew Pearson and Jack Anderson, Simon and Schuster, 1968.

4. Mil Ops, p. 1177.
5. Mil Ops, pp. 1179–1180.
6. Mil Ops, p. 1217.
7. *The New York Times Magazine,* article by James Batten, November 22, 1969.
8. Ibid.
9. *New York Review of Books,* October 23, 1969, p. 10.
10. The rest of the quotations in this chapter are drawn from the Senate Armed Services Committee hearing on the C–5A: SASC Part 2, pp. 1193–2193.

CHAPTER 6, Rivers Delivers

1. *The Nation,* January 19, 1970, p. 43.
2. Column by Mary McGrory in the *Washington Star,* May 22, 1969.
3. *Times,* June 5, 1969. *See also The Nation,* January 19, 1970.
4. Since the House Armed Services Committee does not see fit to provide a usable index to its two-volume, 4360-page hearings, this brief list of witness who testified on the C–5A is presented here, as a source for the rest of the quotations in this chapter:

    May 6: Laird and McConnell .... pp. 2498–2500
    May 7: Seamans and other generals 2577–2601
    May 13: General Jeffrey 2719–2729
    May 20–22: USAF generals 2861–2949
    May 22: Fitzgerald 2949–3037
    June 11: GAO 3037–3070
    June 16: Charles 3071–3101
    June 17: Lockheed 3101–3152

CHAPTER 7, The Ordeal of Ernest Fitzgerald

1. *The New Republic,* August 1, 1970, p. 22.
2. JEC, November, 1969, p. 199.
3. JEC, January, 1969, p. 280.

4. An account of how the Pentagon handled Fitzgerald's material appears in JEC, January, 1969, p. 287.

5. JEC, pp. 325–339.

6. Ibid., pp. 282–286.

7. Ibid., pp. 288–290.

8. HASC, pp. 2591–2592.

9. JEC, November, 1969, pp. 130, 131, 172.

10. JEC, November, 1969, pp. 115–116.

11. *Post,* December 11, 1969.

12. Ibid.

13. The Fitzgerald investigation file was revealed in Jack Anderson's column, *San Francisco Chronicle,* December 26, 1969.

14. JEC, November, 1969, p. 178.

15. *WJS,* December 1, 1970.

CHAPTER 8, The Whittaker Report and Other Ploys

1. *Times,* May 4, 1969.

2. Ibid.

3. *AFJ,* May 10, 1969.

4. *Times,* May 3, 1969.

5. For a summary of the press conference on the Whittaker Report, see *AFJ,* August 2. 1969, p. 21.

6. For a summary of the Whittaker Report, see *Air Force,* September, 1969, pp. 51–55.

7. For a partial list of major subcontractors on the C–5A program, see *Air Force,* April, 1968, p. 76.

CHAPTER 9, The Great Senate Debate

1. *The Nation,* February 9, 1970, p. 137.

2. *Post,* August 31, 1969.

3. HASC, 1969, Part 1, p. 2594.

4. The Senate debate on the C–5A can be found in *The Congressional Record:*

Wednesday, September 3, 1969 .... pp. S10065–S10112
Thursday, September 4, 1969 ....   S10181–S10194
Friday, September 5, 1969 ....   S10231–S10239
Tuesday, September 9, 1969 ....   S10308–S10329
5. *Post,* September 5, 1969.
6. *New York Review of Books,* October 23, 1969, p. 10.
7. Ibid.

CHAPTER 10, Rivers Delivers the House

1. *The Nation,* October 20, 1969, pp. 394–395.
2. The House debate on the C–5A, as well as the entire Fiscal Year
   1970 Military Procurement Bill, appears in *The Congressional
   Record:*
       Wednesday, October 1, 1969 .... pp. H8763–H8816
       Thursday, October 2, 1969 ....   H8847–H8922
3. For an account of the exchanges later deleted from *The Congressional Record,* see *Boston Globe,* October 13, 1969, p. 21.
4. *The Congressional Record,* October 2, 1969, in Extension of Remarks, p. E8093.

CHAPTER 11, The Pentagon Retreats

1. *Post,* September 26, 1969.
2. *AFJ,* November 22, 1969.
3. The Pentagon announcement of the cutback, and Proxmire's response can be found in the *Times,* November 15, 1969.
4. *WSJ,* January 8, 1970.
5. *Post,* January 10, 1970.
6. *AFJ,* December 27, 1969, p. 6; February 21, 1970, p. 6.
7. *AFJ,* July 25, 1970.
8. *WSJ,* February 10, 1970.
9. Ibid.
10. For an analysis of the C–5A's "corollary missions," see *Air Force,*
    April, 1968, p. 97.

CHAPTER 12, Cracked Wings and Other Unforeseen Technical Difficulties

1. JEC, January, 1969, p. 293.
2. Mil Ops, p. 1213.
3. HASC, p. 2723.
4. SASC, p. 2033–2034.
5. SASC, p. 2035.
6. SASC, p. 2083.
7. SASC, p. 2150.
8. JEC, June, 1969, Part 2, pp. 609, 786.
9. Ibid., appendix E, p. 771.
10. *AFJ,* September 6, 1969, p. 53.
11. Ibid., July 26, 1969, p. 13.
12. Ibid., November 1, 1969.
13. *The Congressional Record,* October 1, 1969, p. H8783.
14. Ibid., September 9, 1969, S10326.
15. Ibid., September 3, 1969, p. S10106.
16. Ibid., September 9, 1969, p. S10314.
17. Ibid., September 3, 1969, p. S10069.
18. Ibid., October 2, 1969, p. H8901.
19. Ibid., October 2, 1969, p. H8910.
20. *Post,* December 12, 1969.
21. *The Congressional Record,* December 15, 1969, p. E10690.
22. The Moorhead quotes are from ibid., p. E10691.
23. *Post,* January 20, 1970.
24. *AFJ,* January 24, 1970.
25. *AFJ,* March 28, 1970, p. 9.
26. Ibid.
27. *Post,* May 29, 1970.
28. *AFJ,* May 23, 1970, pp. 12–14.
29. *AFJ,* June 13, 1970, p. 2.
30. Ibid., June 6, 1970, pp. 10–11.
31. Seamans' press conference and the summary of the Bisplinghoff Report can be found in *AFJ,* June 20, 1970, p. 4. The full report appears in *The Congressional Record,* August 13, 1970.

32. *Post,* June 18, 1970.
33. *AFJ,* June 13, 1970, p. 2.
34. The *Boston Globe,* October 18, 1970.

CHAPTER 13, "Stock Market Implications"

 1. Mil Ops, pp. 1179–1182.
 2. HASC, p. 2586.
 3. Ibid.
 4. *Times,* May 3, 1969.
 5. SEC Report, Vol. I, p. 69.
 6. SAC, pp. 2113–2114.
 7. SEC Report, Vol. I, p. 21.
 8. SEC Report, Vol. II, p. 79.
 9. SEC Report, Vol. II, p. 80.
10. *The New Republic,* April 25, 1970, pp. 9–10.
11. SEC Report, Vol. II, p. 80.
12. *Post,* November 7, 1969.
13. Ibid., September 22, 1969.
14. SEC Report, Vol. II, p. 80.
15. *Post,* September 22, 1969.
16. Ibid.
17. Mil Ops, p. 1183.
18. SEC Report, Vol. I, p. 69.
19. *The New Republic,* April 1, 1970, p. 23; April 25, 1970, p. 9.
20. *Times,* September 20, 1970.
21. The SEC announcement and the responses to it can be found in the *Times,* June 3, 1970.
22. SEC Report, Vol. I, p. 4.
23. SEC Report, Vol. II, pp. 79–82.
24. Ibid., p. 80.
25. Ibid., p. 18.
26. Ibid., p. 64.
27. Ibid., p. 78.
28. Ibid., p. 63.
29. Ibid., p. 67.

30. Ibid., Vol. I, p. 8.
31. Ibid., p. 54.
32. Ibid., p. 4.
33. Ibid., p. 31.
34. Ibid., p. 36.
35. Ibid., p. 38.
36. Ibid., p. 43.
37. Ibid., pp. 58–60.
38. Ibid., p. 57–58.
39. HASC, p. 2982.
40. SEC Report, Vol. I, p. 43.
41. *AFJ,* July 18, 1970, p. 9.

CHAPTER 14, A Small Matter of $500 Million

1. HASC, p. 2937.
2. SASC, p. 2190.
3. JEC, January, 1970, pp. 256–257.
4. The report on the May, 1969, progress payments and Senator Byrd's quote can be found in SASC, p. 2176.
5. JEC, January, 1970.
6. The report on the milestone payments and Senator Proxmire's quote can be found in JEC, January, 1970, p. 277.
7. *The Congressional Record,* September 9, 1969, pp. S10327–S10328.
8. Senator Proxmire's letter to Whittaker, dated February 26, 1970, is unpublished.
9. *AFJ,* March 14, 1970, pp. 22–23.
10. *Fortune,* September, 1970.
11. The Pike and Moorhead quotes can be found in the *Post,* March 6, 1970.
12. Ibid., March 7, 1970.
13. *AFJ,* March 21, 1970, p. 21.
14. The defense contractor's quote and the note on letters can be found in *AFJ,* April 4, 1970, p. 6.
15. *WSJ,* March 10, 1970.

228 THE C–5A SCANDAL

16. Ibid.
17. *Newsweek,* March 16, 1970, p. 89.
18. Ibid.
19. For an account of Packard's testimony to the HASC, see the *Times,* March 10, 1970, and *WSJ,* March 10, 1970.
20. *AFJ,* April 11, 1970, p. 9.
21. *WSJ,* May 21, 1970.
22. Ibid.
23. *Post,* May 29, 1970.
24. *AFJ,* March 12, 1970, p. 4, and March 21, 1970, p. 6.
25. *The New Republic,* March 28, 1970, p. 8.
26. *Post,* March 7, 1970.
27. Interview with author.
28. *WSJ,* May 28, 1970; *AFJ,* June 6, 1970, pp. 10–11.
29. *AFJ,* March 14, 1970, p. 13.
30. *The Nation,* April 6, 1970.
31. HASC, p. 2500.
32. *Post,* May 29, 1970.
33. *Post,* April 29, 1970.
34. *AFJ,* May 9, 1970, p. 7.
35. *Times,* September 12, 1970.
36. *The New Republic,* October 10, 1970, pp. 11–13.

CHAPTER 15, What Everyone Learned From the C–5A

1. *Times,* May 6, 1970.
2. *Times,* April 12, 1970.
3. *AFJ,* March 14, 1970, pp. 22–23.
4. *Times,* May 6, 1970.
5. *Air Force,* February, 1970, p. 16.
6. *AFJ,* October 11, 1970.
7. *Air Force,* op. cit.
8. JEC, June, 1969, p. 548; *AFJ,* September 27, 1969; *Post,* December 25, 1969.
9. *Air Force,* September, 1970, p. 27.

10. *Times,* June 10, 1970.
11. *Times,* December 11, 1969.
12. *The Nation,* April 6, 1970.
13. Information on the fiscal 1971 budget can be found in *Armed Forces Management,* April, 1970, p. 48.
14. *AFJ,* February 1, 1970, p. 10.
15. *Times,* December 29, 1970.
16. Interview with author.
17. *Baltimore News American,* May 9, 1969.
18. Ibid.
19. *Government Executive,* September, 1969, pp. 15–16.
20. Ibid.
21. *Barrons,* August 17, 1970, p. 1.
22. *Times,* July 30, 1970.
23. *Baltimore News American,* May 9, 1969.
24. Ibid.
25. *The Nation,* November 30, 1957.
26. HASC, p. 3007.
27. *Baltimore News American,* May 9, 1969.
28. Interview with author.
29. The report on the DSRV and the GAO study can be found in *AFJ,* June 21, 1969.
30. *Report from Wasteland: America's Military Industrial Complex,* by Senator William Proxmire (New York: Praeger, 1970), pp. 17–18.
31. Mil Ops, Part 5, p. 1411.
32. *Post,* January 6, 1970.
33. Ibid., June 12, 1969.
34. Interview with author.
35. *AFJ,* February 21, 1970, p. 18.
36. *The Congressional Record,* September 9, 1969, S10316.

Index

Business Week, quoted, 48
"buying-in," defined, 18–19. *See
also* C–5A cost and overrun;
Lockheed

C–5A Galaxy
CONSTRUCTION AND PERFORM-
ANCE: size, features, and capabilities, 1–3; Lockheed contract design change, 10; early
technical problems, 29–32; Air
Force "cure notice," 30–31;
use of British engineers, 31;
roll-out ceremony, 41–42; first
flight, 43; Air Force claims
about performance, 146–149;
reduction of performance standards, 149–150; Whittaker Report, 150–151; wing problems,
151–152, 156, 158; House debate on C–5A defects, 153–
154; GAO report on performance problems, 154–155; delivery, 155–157; radar system
problems, 157; Bisplinghoff
Report, 157–161; landing ac-
cidents, 161–162; explosion of
first C–5A, 162
CONTRACT: bidding and competition for, 5–7, 9–10, 12–15;
lobbying by Lockheed, 12–15;
decision and award of, 16–17;
"buying-in" by Lockheed, 18–
19, 27–28, 85–86, 208–209;
and Charles, 21–28; Total
Package Procurement, 23–25,
30, 197, 200; McNamara
praise for, 23; terms of, 24–
26; option for Run B, 24–26,
46–52, 79, 140–141, 179;
schedule delays, 25, 142; "cure
notice," 30–31; contract
changes, 31–32, 149–150; and
Brown, 33; Seamans on, 69;

spare parts, 82–83; cutback,
140–141; dispute over, 141,
182–183, 186, 194–195; progress payments, 179–180; milestone payments, 180
COST AND OVERRUN: bidding, 6–
7, 10, 25, 27; "buying-in," 18–
19, 27–28, 85–86, 208–209;
Total Package Procurement,
23–25; cost incentive, 25; and
repricing formula, 25–27, 33,
45, 49–51, 79, 108, 179; effect of construction problems
on, 29–33; budget increases,
32–33, 38, 41, 179; Fitzgerald
reports and testimony on, 32–
33, 35, 45, 61, 81–82, 140;
concealment by Lockheed, 35,
168–170, 174–176; reports by
Col. Killpack and Col. Warren, 35–36; and Gen. Crow,
37; and Gen. McConnell, 38;
and Anthony, 38, 208; dispute
between Air Force and Lockheed, 39, 72; concealment by
Air Force, 39–40, 46, 62–63,
70–71, 77–81, 88, 140–141;
and Charles, 40–41, 56–57,
63–64, 84–86; GAO investigation, 45–50, 82–83; compared
to 747, 55–56, 135, 192; spare
parts, 57, 82–83, 91; Seamans
estimate, 68; and Rivers, 81;
Senate debate on, 116–117,
122, 125–126; and Proxmire,
116–117; cost per ton-mile,
120–121; Pike estimate of unit
cost, 135; estimate of Lockheed loss, 141; USAF estimate
for cost of wing "fix," 157;
Lockheed request for $500
million, 181–182; "contingency fund," 191–194
DEFENSE POLICY: original strategic conception, 3–4; "remote